ROCK**GUITAR** **MODE**MASTERY

A Guide to Learning and Applying the Modes
to Rock and Shred Metal Guitar with Chris Zoupa

CHRIS**ZOUPA**

FUNDAMENTAL**CHANGES**

Rock Guitar Mode Mastery

A Guide to Learning and Applying the Modes to Rock and Shred Metal Guitar with Chris Zoupa

Published by **www.fundamental-changes.com**

ISBN 978-1-78933-015-1

Edited by Tim Pettingale

www.fundamental-changes.com

Twitter: **@guitar_joseph**

Over 10,000 fans on Facebook: **FundamentalChangesInGuitar**

Instagram: **FundamentalChanges**

For over 350 Free Guitar Lessons with Videos Check Out

www.fundamental-changes.com

Cover Image Copyright: Chris Zoupa used by permission

Contents

Foreword

I started teaching guitar when I was 15 years old. I talked to a couple of other kids at school about, "Comin' 'round for a shred." My sales pitch consisted of, "Yeah, I teach" and "Yeah, I can show you some stuff!" I also put an ad in the school newsletter that read:

Rock and Metal Guitar Lessons. 1st LESSON FREE!

Eventually the phone rang, with someone *actually enquiring* about guitar lessons.

Initially, I was freaked out about the idea of people paying ME to teach them guitar. The reality was, I was untrained, I lacked knowledge, and had little understanding of how to pass on information. Basically, I was going to have to wing it. But I got lucky. I found that I had a knack for it and fell in love with teaching straight away. Of course, like most young teachers, the early years consisted of fooling around with Metallica, Megadeth, Slayer and Guns N' Roses riffs – all the fun stuff.

When I was about 19, theory, improvisation and composition started to interest me and I became infatuated with the modes. The more I used them, and the more epiphanies I had, the more I wanted to teach them and share what I believed to be "amazing discoveries". I didn't care who it was, I just needed someone to share my excitement with – even if it was one of the tiny kids who could barely hold a guitar.

Now, as a gentleman of thirty-one and a half years (insert adult level sigh here), I decided to write a book to help those who want a "plain English" guide to the modes. A book that would show guitar players how to use the modes in context, without the fear of playing wrong notes or, worse, having a spontaneous head explosion. I've lost count of the number of times I've begun naming the modes to a student, saying "Mixolydian" or "Locrian", and they've looked at me as if to say, "I'm sorry, sir. I did not realise I was paying for an astrophysics class taught in ancient Aramaic!"

I'm hoping that this book will remove your fear of new, scary words, and give you the confidence and understanding to apply modal music theory. The moment you start understanding the modes and their theoretical application is an exciting and liberating one. It will have a great effect on your composition of chord progressions, riffs, solo writing, and how you approach improvisation.

Did someone say, "That's a good place to throw in a m7b5 arpeggio"?!

Alas, let's get learning.

Chris

Get the Audio

The audio files for this book are available to download for free from **www.fundamental-changes.com.** The link is in the top right-hand corner. Simply select this book title from the drop-down menu and follow the instructions to get the audio.

We recommend that you download the files directly to your computer, not to your tablet, and extract them there before adding them to your media library. You can then put them on your tablet, iPod or burn them to CD. On the download page there is a help PDF, and we also provide technical support via the contact form.

Kindle / eReaders

To get the most out of this book, remember that you can **double tap any image to enlarge it**. Turn off 'column viewing' and hold your Kindle in landscape mode.

For over 350 Free Guitar Lessons with Videos Check out:

www.fundamental-changes.com

Twitter: **@guitar_joseph**

Over 10,000 fans on Facebook: **FundamentalChangesInGuitar**

Instagram: **FundamentalChanges**

Get your audio now for free:

It makes the book come alive, and you'll learn much more!

www.fundamental-changes.com/download-audio

An Introduction to Modes

Since the dawn of time, modes have freaked people out – especially guitarists. The pretentious and pompous musicians of the world have used their modal knowledge to look down smugly from their pedestals and dismiss the rest of us "theory-less, self-taught peasants" and make us feel all the more basic and pedestrian.

Before we delve too far down the theory rabbit hole, we need to be able to understand and answer a very simple question: *what is a mode?* We need to understand their purpose, and their theoretical and practical application, so we can use them to make awesome music.

Put simply, a mode is a scale derived from the notes of a parent scale. For example, given the parent scale of C Major (C D E F G A B), the second mode will consist of the notes D E F G A B C. The third mode will consist of the notes E F G A B C D, and so on.

A major scale is always built from a set pattern of tones and semitones. Looking at our C Major scale we can see that,

C to D = Tone

D to E = Tone

E to F = Semitone

F to G = Tone

G to A = Tone

A to B = Tone

B to C = Semitone

(notated for convenience as T T St T T T St)

When we start from a different note in the scale to create a mode, we create a different pattern of tones and semitones. For example, it we begin with a D note we get,

D to E = Tone

E to F = Semitone

F to G = Tone

G to A = Tone

A to B = Tone

B to C = Semitone

C to D = Tone

(T **St T** T T St T)

This pattern of tones and semitones sound *very* different from the pattern of tones and semitones in our original C Major scale. So just by playing a major scale beginning on a different note, we can create a whole different mood in music very easily.

This can be tricky to hear when simply playing an isolated sequence of notes (from D to D, or E to E, for example). However, when we *harmonise* (make chords out of) the modes, and play over progressions built from chords in the mode, they quickly take on very distinct personalities. We have the funky chilled out jazz of the Dorian mode (D to D), the country-blues of the Mixolydian (G to G), and the dark, dislocating dissonance of the Locrian (B to B).

Modes are used to convey different moods, feelings and textures. They are often used to create a precise sound or mood that characterises a specific musical genre. Modes can even be used to create a sound evocative of certain time periods, countries, religions or cultures.

In this book we'll cover the seven "church" modes of Ionian, Dorian, Phrygian, Lydian, Mixolydian, Aeolian and Locrian. Every mode we discuss will be compared to its parent major scale, to help you understand why it sounds different.

By now, you're probably asking yourself,

"How does playing a scale using the exact same notes, but in a different, order create a different sound?"

That's a solid question.

One simple way to understand it is that, although we are using the same seven notes, the "home base" is different for each mode. The home base is the note the scale begins and ends on. There is also a home base chord to go with it, that the mode works beautifully over. So, even though the notes are the same, the change of home base means that they function differently. In fact, the notes have varying degrees of importance from one mode to the next.

Let's explore this a bit further:

In the key of C Major, the home base note is C and the home base chord is C Major. The *strong* chord sounds in C Major are C Major, F Major and G Major. Every melodic lick or line you play is heard in relation to these strong chords and your ears interpret them as "happy".

If we begin from the second note in the C Major scale (D), we are now in D Dorian. The home base note is D and the home base chord is D Minor. The *strong* chord sounds in this mode are D Minor, G Major (or G7) and A Minor. Every melody you play is heard in relation to these strong chords (normally the first, fourth and fifth chords in the harmonised scale) and suddenly your melodies sound completely different. Even though you are playing all the same notes as the C Major scale, now your ears interpret them as "sad" or "melancholy" because you hear all the scale notes in relation to different strong chords.

Each mode has its own character and mood and the chords produced by each mode are like the colour of a wall where you hang a painting. The same painting can evoke a different mood, just because it's hanging on a different coloured wall.

Now we're going to explore the modes. We'll start off by learning each one over one octave to establish an immediate understanding of its characteristic sound and intervals. Then we'll dive in deep for a thorough analysis with lots of example licks to learn.

Chapter 1: Owning your Ionian

The beginning of one's modal journey can be a terrifying one. It is a quest riddled with new and scary words, accompanied by the unjust pomposity of that one jazz nerd who loves to think they have something over you!

Now that we've looked at the basics of modal theory, we're going to explore the *sound* of each mode in turn and learn some licks that highlight its unique flavour. I'll also suggests some songs you can listen to, based around each mode.

Let's start at square one and talk about the Ionian mode. Known for its happy, joyous nature, the Ionian mode is often used to create uplifting moments in classical music and film scores. It has been used in children's nursery rhymes and lullabies for centuries, and has made frequent appearances in pop music for the last 60+ years.

Don't let this mystical new word fool you – you've already heard this mode close to a Bajillion times in your lifetime.

DISCLAIMER: "Bajillion" is not a real number and I have no science to back up my previous statement.

Part 1: Finding the Ionian sound

The Ionian mode is the first of the seven diatonic modes and is often referred to simply as "the major scale". It's predominantly used to convey a sense of triumph and joy and you will have heard it used repeatedly in modern and classic pop music. It's the happiest sounding of the seven modes and is the easiest to identify.

The Major scale is the basis of all the "rules" of music that have been around for hundreds of years. It's the yardstick by which all other scales are described and, as such, it's given a very simple formula.

Starting on any note on the guitar and ascending using the pattern "Tone Tone Semitone Tone Tone Tone Semitone" will form a major scale. This pattern of notes is given the formula 1 2 3 4 5 6 7

Let's look at the sound and characteristics of the Ionian mode. Listen carefully to the relationship between the notes and think about what mood the scale conveys. Here's a reminder of the Ionian mode in one octave in the key of C Major. Try playing it over the C Ionian backing track.

C Ionian: C D E F G A B C

Example 1a:

The intervals (distances between each note) of the Ionian scale are T T St T T T St (T = Tone; St = Semitone).

The scale formula for the Ionian mode is 1 2 3 4 5 6 7

Tip: As we progress, try to memorise the intervals for each mode. This will help you to differentiate each mode's characteristics, emotions and superpowers!

In any mode, the 3rd interval defines whether it is major or minor. A Major 3rd (four semitones) tells us that the scale is major and will have a happy quality to it. A Minor 3rd (also known as a b3 = three semitones) tells us that the scale is minor and will have a sad quality.

Apart from the 3rd, the most important "character" intervals of the Ionian mode are its 4th and 7th. These notes distinguish it from the Lydian and Mixolydian modes (the two other major modes that contain a major 3rd).

It is difficult to hear the unique qualities of a mode when playing it in isolation. We can get a better feel for its character if we hear it played over a simple progression built from the chords of the mode.

Example 1b is an Ionian chord progression. First play through the chords, then play the ascending and descending versions of the scale. Try playing the scale over the C Major backing track provided and create your own melodies. Listen to which notes sound tense and which notes sound resolved.

Example 1b: C Ionian chord progression and scale ascending & descending

The combination of these chords, even without the scale runs, is enough to create the happy, joyous Ionian signature sound, because they contain important notes of the scale. Painting a modal "picture" isn't just about the notes of the scale – it's about the chords and harmonies that occur within the scale, and the interplay of melody against those chords.

Tip: a dedicated study of music theory, scale shapes, and note/interval knowledge will certainly make you a more *learned* player, but nothing beats understanding the melodic sound and feel that a mode creates. This is something internal to you as a player – you can't write it down on a piece of paper and play it on the fretboard.

Here are some well-known songs built around the Ionian mode for you to go and check out:

*   Better Be Home Soon – Crowded House

*   Let It Be – The Beatles

*   You And Me – Lifehouse

*   Stand By Me – Ben E. King

*   Runaway – The Corrs

Listen carefully to how these songs sound and see if you can identify and add other songs to the list.

Part 2: Diatonic Chords

I've mentioned that each mode has certain chords that belong to it, and now we'll look at how to construct them. "Diatonic chords" simply refers to chords that are built from each degree of the scale. Understanding which chords belong to which mode will help massively when you come use them in a musical context.

Remember that the notes of C Ionian are C D E F G A B.

To form a chord, we simply stack alternate notes from the scale. For example, we start on C and take the 1st, 3rd and 5th notes (C E G), and play them together to form a C Major chord.

(C) D **(E)** F **(G)** A B C

Next, we move to the note D and treat it as our "1". The 1st, 3rd and 5th notes (D F A), played together form a D Minor chord.

Repeating this process for every note of the C Major results in the following chords:

C major (C E G)

D minor (D F A)

E minor (E G B)

F major (F A C)

G major (G B D)

A minor (A C E)

B minor7b5 (B D F A)

In "proper music theory" (I know, snore-fest), each chord is given a Roman numeral to identify it. The Roman numerals are normally displayed as upper case for major chords and lower case for minor chords.

Taking each note of the Ionian mode in turn, the harmonised scale is as follows:

I	ii	iii	IV	V	vi	vii
maj	min	min	maj	maj	min	min7b5 (or 1/2 diminished)

Here they are played as simple open chords:

Example 1c:

These chords should be familiar to you as they are foundational to guitar playing and make up the majority of "beginner" guitar songs. Try writing a few chord progressions with them, preferably beginning and ending on a C major chord, so that you get a feel for the Ionian sound. Here are a couple of examples:

Example 1d – progression 1:

Example 1e – progression 2:

Part 3: Soloing in Ionian using scales and arpeggios

I've probably said this thousands of times over the years to students: "In the beginning, it's often hard to know where to start when soloing modally." So to make things easier, before I start writing or improvising, I ask myself these questions:

1. What is the three-note-per-string pattern for this mode from the root?

2. What kind of pentatonic scales are hiding in the mode. E.g. regular, custom or relative minor?

3. What types of arpeggios will bring out the flavour of the mode?

Let's look at each of these in turn before learning a load of cool licks that use each approach.

First, let's take the simple Ionian scale from the start of the chapter and stretch it across six strings with a three-note-per-string pattern.

Example 1f:

This is the fastest way to play and hear the mode across two and a bit octaves. As a pattern, it's also fairly easy to use in composition and improvisation. Learn it over the C Major backing track.

Pentatonics

Another effective way of playing the Ionian mode is to take just five of its seven notes and turn them into a pentatonic scale. The major pentatonic scale is made up from the 1st (C), 2nd (D), 3rd (E), 5th (G) and 6th (A) notes of the Ionian scale. Having five notes instead of seven means there are fewer notes between the root and the octave, which creates wider intervals and allows us to make bigger harmonic jumps. Let's take a look at that scale in a box-shaped pattern.

Example 1g:

If you feel the box pattern is too restrictive, you can use a crawling pentatonic shape that works diagonally across the neck.

Example 1h:

Side note: C Major Pentatonic and A Minor Pentatonic share identical notes, just played in a different order:

C Major Pentatonic = C D E G A

A Minor Pentatonic = A C D E G

This means you can use them interchangeably. If you are playing in C Ionian or A Aeolian, both shapes can be used over both modes. Here they are side by side:

Example 1i:

If you're more comfortable with the minor pentatonic shape, use that one instead. Remember that you can use your original three-note-per-string shape and the pentatonic scale shape to mix things up and break the monotony of running up and down one pattern.

Arpeggios

Another cool way to emphasise the sound of the Ionian mode is to use major triad arpeggios. (These are the simple chords we made earlier: C major – C E G, D minor – D F A, etc). We can also add a fourth note to these triads to create a major 7th arpeggio (Cmaj7 has the notes C E G B). Example 1j illustrates how the triad arpeggio (made from the 1st, 3rd and 5th notes of C Ionian) sounds compared to the major 7th arpeggio (1st, 3rd, 5th and 7th).

Example 1j:

Example 1k:

Experiment with both arpeggios. Straight triads can sound a little predictable. Overuse the major 7th, however, and it can sound too jazzy.

You can play both triad and major 7th arpeggios in a lower register with different shapes:

Learning more arpeggio positions gives you more options and means you can shift between endless ideas that span the fretboard. Listen to the multiple arpeggio inversions of the same chord used on Jason Becker's masterpiece album, *Perpetual Burn*. The title track has an amazing sequence of arpeggios joined together at 1:41.

Lastly, I want to show you my two favourite ways to play a major 7th arpeggio so that it spans all six strings. This first shape leads from the major 7th (B) then plays the 1st, 3rd and 5th scale intervals. There's a slide in the middle of the arpeggio to help position the hand for the major triad. It also helps the arpeggio sound less robotic and more like a phrase.

Example 1l:

The second shape also leads from the major 7th and works across three octaves. This shape is more predictable as each octave is played identically. I've seen guitarists like Marty Friedman (Megadeth, Cacophony) and Corey Beaulieu of Trivium use this shape spectacularly in a few solos!

Example 1m:

Experiment with different patterns using this arpeggio. You don't always have to lead from the seventh or the root note. Your main consideration should be how what you're playing sounds over the backing chords and key signature.

Tip: These shapes work equally well in a Lydian context. That means you can play them over a I chord (Ionian) or IV chord (Lydian) in any chord progression.

OK, here's the bit you've been waiting for, let's learn some of my favourite Ionian licks.

Part 4: Ionian licks to help you get creative

I've given you some useful scales and arpeggio shapes already, and at this point you might be thinking, "Thanks Chris, that's all I need!" However, you may then sit down to improvise and everything you'd play would sound linear and robotic – boring runs or, worse, up-and-down arpeggios! At which point you'd say to yourself, "That evil jerk face! Chris lied to us. He lied to all of us – even the sooty orphans at CHRISTMAS no less!"

Firstly, calm down! Secondly, I haven't properly shown you how to get the most out of those ideas yet. For the final part of this chapter, I've prepared several Ionian licks to show you how to bring these melodic ideas together in an expressive way in a musical context.

The first lick I want to show you is a major pentatonic pattern, crawling across the neck, using slides and hammer-ons to add flavour. Play all the ideas in this section over the C Ionian backing track.

Example 1n: Sliding C Major pentatonic lick

I'm a massive fan of licks like this that encourage you to use the whole neck of the guitar and force you to execute positions shifts. They can help you break out of rigid box patterns and can be used to transition from one position to the next.

In the next example, we'll use position 1 of the A Minor pentatonic, then shift up the neck.

Example 1o: A Minor pentatonic drifting positions lick

This is a relatively simple idea. I decided to target and rest briefly on the C note – the root note of a C Major chord. However, you could also target the major 3rd (E) or 5th (G) to support the chord. Your target notes will change if you play this lick over a different chord in the progression, so tinker with it accordingly. Try using this lick to drift from one minor pentatonic position to the next.

Example 1p uses the C Ionian three-note-per-string scale shape. It ascends in triplets, but varies between 1/8th and 1/16th notes to add an occasional burst of speed. I use this approach a lot in improvisation and composition. I've seen Mark Tremonti play similar licks in a few Alter Bridge solos.

Example 1p: Tremonti-style diatonic building lick

After playing through this lick a few times, you'll notice that the addition of speed variance and legato are a great way to break up the monotony of a linear ascending scale run. It's also really interesting to switch between legato technique and shredding in the same lick. This lick can also be applied to any three-note-per-string modal shape.

Side note: I may go into detail about more exotic, adventurous modes in a future book. It'll need to have a sassy yet bold name. Until then, let's keep it simple. There's also a very good chance Jens Larsen will write that book before me and do a very good job. SIGH! (Seriously though, check out Jens Larsen on YouTube).

Example 1q combines old school, Chuck Berry-influenced blues rock pentatonics with a few additional scale notes to give a nice mix of both scales. This lick starts with a D note bent a full tone to E. It also ends on an E note to highlight the major 3rd of the C Major chord.

Guitar legends Carlos Santana and Slash use this concept to create moments of triumphant rocking out, mixed with powerful emotion. It's a great way to blend the rocky-blues sound of the pentatonic with the heartstring-pulling emotion of the diatonic scale. The pentatonic scale is completely devoid of semitones – the most emotional sounding of intervals – which is why borrowing diatonic scale notes can be so effective. Think of it as having your rock cake and emotionally eating it!

Example 1q: Chuck Berry A pentatonic lick with diatonic descending notes

The next example lick uses a G pedal note, while the other notes work diatonically through C Ionian. This kind of lick is cool because it creates tension and has movement, yet the pedal makes it seem as though it's not moving much at all. Players such as John Mayer, Mikael Akerfeldt and Alex Skolnick have used this concept very subtly in some of their solos.

Example 1r: C Ionian pedal note lick

This next idea combines an arpeggio with some passing notes. It's a simple C Major triad (C E G), but I've added a F on the turnaround for extra flavour. Notice that I've also added a slide from D# to E before descending the arpeggio. This "outside" note adds further tension as it doesn't belong to the C Ionian mode. You can use this idea in scales too, not just in arpeggios. Just make sure you move from the outside note (sometimes referred to as a WRONG note) to a scale note – preferably one that supports the chords you are playing over.

Example 1s: Five string C Major arpeggio lick with outside note slide

Example 1t has an ascending Cmaj7 arpeggio over three octaves, spanning all six strings, and uses a hammer-on on every string. Descending, we have diatonic notes from C Ionian.

Example 1t: Six-string Cmaj7 arpeggio with descending diatonic legato lick

You may have noticed there are several position shifts in this lick. The shifts help avoid this becoming a linear, predictable sounding run.

The next lick uses position three of the A Minor pentatonic scale and ascends in groups of five, using legato technique. There's a sliding position shift into a descending Cmaj7 arpeggio.

Example 1u: A Minor pentatonic with five-note groupings and string skip descending Cmaj7 arpeggio

Did you notice the multiple slides in that lick? I'd like to point out that SLIDES ARE YOUR FRIEND. Not only is sliding a useful, expressive technique, it can also make position shifts seamless and less clunky.

Example 1v uses the first position of the A Minor pentatonic scale, but is played with many string skips. Pay attention to the legato emphasis and be wary of the complications that can occur during string skips!

Example 1v: String skipped legato A Minor pentatonic lick with minor 6th and b5 notes

One cool thing you may have noticed is that string skips create less predictable intervals. It's a very basic trick to make the delivery of a scale or arpeggio more interesting. This intervallic approach need not be limited to the pentatonic, however – it's useable in all scales and modes.

The final example of this chapter uses the three-note-per-string C Ionian scale shape again. It uses a rolling legato technique descending, while adding a few tapped notes which are diatonic to the scale. This adds flavour and a degree of surprise.

Example 1w: C Ionian descending legato lick with taps

It's important to remember that all the C Ionian ideas you've learnt can be modulated to other Ionian keys. Find some jam tracks in different keys to practise over and try your best to nail that happy, cheery major Ionian sound with the notes you play. If your audience is smiling, you're doing it right!

Chapter 2: Deciphering Dorian

Our modal journey continues and we venture into the void of Dorian. This mode is an absolute delight to listen to and play, as it highlights some sexy aspects of minor modality. Yet, it has some of the uplifting qualities of the major too. An extremely versatile mode, it is found in multiple music genres including country, jazz, blues, fusion and lots of RnB.

Dorian is classed as a minor mode due to its b3 interval. Remember that in a scale or chord, 3 = major, b3 = minor.

Dorian is the second of the seven diatonic modes. I often refer to it as "a minor scale with a sense of hope" or "the Pink Floyd mode". Pink Floyd used the Dorian mode poignantly and tastefully to stir great emotion in songs like *The Great Big Gig in the Sky* and *Shine on You Crazy Diamond.*

This mode is also used to great effect in the soundtrack to *The Hobbit* and all of the *Lord of the Rings* films – often to underline the trouble and adversity the hobbits will face, along with their ability to overcome it with the power of friendship and determination.

Dorian is commonly used in jazz, fusion and sometimes rock music. The only thing that differentiates it from the more common and traditional Aeolian mode is that the Dorian scale has a *natural* 6th note (often referred to as the major 6th) and Aeolian has a b6. This single note is the only difference between Dorian and Aeolian, but it makes a huge difference in sound. Really! The difference a single note can make is unbelievable! We haven't even got to Lydian yet… that'll blow you away!

Part 1: Finding the Dorian sound

Let's begin by listening to the sound of this mode in a simple, one octave format. Again, listen out for the relationship between the intervals which yield its distinctive sound. Pay attention as well to the mood it creates and think about how you can convey this in your music.

In this chapter we will switch to the key of F Major and use G Dorian for all the examples.

Let's take a look at the G Dorian scale played to one octave.

Example 2a:

While it's important to learn Dorian as a sound in its own right, in the back of your mind it's important to know that the Dorian mode is just like the Aeolian mode but with a natural 6th. In the diagram below we have G Aeolian and G Dorian side by side.

Example 2b:

Aeolian scale formula = 1 2 b3 4 5 b6 b7

Dorian scale formula = 1 2 b3 4 5 6 b7

As the Aeolian is the most common minor mode, it's a useful yardstick to help describe the other minor modes (Dorian, Phrygian, and Locrian), just as the Ionian is a great yardstick for the major modes.

The b3 gives the Dorian its minor sound, making it sound sad, but its natural 6th injects an uplifting, hopeful undertone, so it's definitely not as sombre as the Aeolian. The Aeolian has a semitone interval between the fifth and sixth notes, whereas the Dorian has a full tone. It's this full tone "character" note that produces its signature sound – a small injection of hope. Though it's a subtle difference, the natural 6th is more positive sounding than the melancholy minor 6th of the Aeolian.

Though comparing the two scales is a great way to see how they differ, it doesn't give us enough of an understanding of how Dorian will work in context over music. Play through this simple two-chord progression and then play through the ascending and descending versions of the scale. Then try it over the G Dorian backing track.

Example 2c: G Dorian chord progression with scale ascend & descend

Scale Runs

You will notice that the characteristic 6th note (E) reacts with the Gm7 chord to create a Gm6 sound. Gm6 is made up of G, Bb, D and E, and has that characteristically Dorian sound.

The E note is also present as the major 3rd in the C9 chord, which is made up of C, E, Bb and D. We can hear the interplay between the chords and the scale creating a sombre minor feel that's followed immediately by a hopeful major lift. This is a very simple way to create an understanding of the Dorian sound and how you feel when you hear it.

Here are some reference songs that contain the characteristic Dorian sound:

- The Unforgiven – Metallica

- Mad World – Tears For Fears

- Wicked Game – Chris Isaak

- The Extremist – Joe Satriani

- Whatta Man – Salt N' Pepa

Part 2: The Dorian diatonic chords

As discussed, it's important to understand the diatonic chords belonging to each mode because it helps us to determine how to highlight the mode's colour and emotion. Let's look at the diatonic chords of the Dorian mode compared to the Ionian mode.

Diatonic chords built from Ionian:

maj	min	min	maj	maj	min	min7b5
I	ii	iii	IV	V	vi	vii

Diatonic chords built from Dorian:

min	min	maj	maj	min	min7b5	maj
i	ii	bIII	IV	v	vi	bVII

The previous diagram shows that the first chord of the harmonised Dorian scale is minor, whereas in Ionian it's major. The first (tonic) chord is always the most important in defining the mood of the scale, so you can already see that Dorian and Ionian will sound very different. What other differences can you spot in the harmonised scale?

In the same way that we built chords by harmonising the Ionian mode, we can do the same with the Dorian mode to give us the G Dorian chord structure:

Example 2d:

When composing using a mode, we want to choose chords that reflect its characteristic sound. In the case of the Dorian, we can highlight that natural 6th. The natural 6th (an E note in the key of G Dorian) occurs in the chords C Major, Am and Em7b5.

C Major (IV chord) = C E G

Am (ii chord) = A C E

Em7b5 (vi chord) = E G Bb D

Of course, we normally want to include the tonic chord (Gm) too!

Try composing some Dorian chord progressions of your own, keeping in mind to highlight the characteristic sound of the mode. Try to begin and end with a Gm chord. Here are a couple of suggestions to start you off:

Example 2e – Progression 1:

Example 2f – Progression 2:

Part 3: Soloing in Dorian with scales and arpeggios

The early stages of modal improvisation and composition can be daunting and it's often hard to know where to begin. My approach to solo writing and improvisation using the Dorian mode uses the same checklist as the previous chapter:

1. What is the three-note-per-string pattern for this mode from the root?

2. What kind of pentatonics can I use e.g. regular, custom or relative minor?

3. What kinds of arpeggios will bring out the flavour of the mode?

First, let's take our G Dorian scale from the start of this chapter and stretch it across six strings with a three-note-per-string pattern. Try it over the Dorian backing track.

Example 2g:

This is the quickest way to hear the Dorian mode working across two and a bit octaves. It's also a good shape to use for solos if you're new to the Dorian. When improvising, I like to highlight:

* The b3rd (Bb in the case of G Dorian) – it's what gives it its sadder, melancholy sound

* The major 6th (E in G Dorian) – it's the most flavoursome note; the natural 6th note gives this scale its bittersweet quality – an unexpected lift you don't find in typical minor scales.

Pentatonics

Let's talk pentatonics – *ye olde faithful* of scales for improvisation. Dorian is a minor mode, so we can play it using regular minor pentatonic patterns made up from the 1st, 3rd, 4th, 5th and 7th degrees of the scale.

Omitting the 2nd and 6th degrees is a smart thing to do, because it leaves us with "neutral" notes that can work in other modal contexts (Aeolian and Phrygian) as well as Dorian. Here is G Dorian starting from the root, expressed as the familiar pentatonic shape we all know and love.

Example 2h:

This simple shape won't sound out of place over any Dorian chord progression, but let's hear it again, adding in that characteristic major 6th note (E). This is so easy to do, but adds so much expression.

Example 2i:

I use this latter shape all the time. You can hear the full effect of adding in the major 6th note when jamming over a Dorian chord progression. Below I've illustrated the other four positions of our pentatonic scale. For each position there is a version without, then with the major 6th, so you can really hear the difference.

Example 2j:

Position 2 Gm Pentatonic

Position 2 Gm Pentatonic + major 6th

Position 3 Gm Pentatonic

Position 3 Gm Pentatonic + major 6th

Position 4 Gm Pentatonic

Position 4 Gm Pentatonic + major 6th

Position 5 Gm Pentatonic

Position 5 Gm Pentatonic + major 6th

Arpeggios

Now let's accentuate the Dorian flavour using arpeggios. Example 2k illustrates a basic G Minor arpeggio with added major 6th.

Side note/stunning fact: The basic G Minor triad consists of the notes G, Bb and D. The addition of the major 6th (E) turns it into a Gm6. Coincidentally, Gm6 shares all the same notes as Em7b5 (E half-diminished). If you're struggling to play something over a pesky Em7b5 chord, G Dorian works amazingly well.

Example 2k:

This works to perfectly highlight the i or vi chords in a Dorian progression, but also works well used casually over a droning Dorian riff. We could also use a Gm7 arpeggio (G Bb D F) and add in the E again:

Example 2l:

These arpeggios with the special major 6th will sound good over a ii minor chord in any key. And don't forget your Dorian secret weapon when confronted with a m7b5 chord. Dorian is a very versatile mode and can be used in many musical situations.

Part 4: Dorian licks to help you get creative

I've prepared a few licks in G Dorian based on the diatonic and pentatonic scale shapes we've discussed, as well as some arpeggios. These will help you to see how the Dorian can be applied melodically in an expressive, musical context.

The first example uses a simple G Minor pentatonic lick with a cheeky bend from the E note. This is a great way to highlight the natural 6th while keeping things bluesy. Players like Stevie Ray Vaughn, David Gilmour and Joe Bonamassa use this approach frequently when a Dorian situation presents itself.

Example 2m: Bluesy lick with Dorian 6th

This kind of lick works well over the i chord (Gm) in a Dorian progression, but is also compatible with the IV chord (C7) as it highlights the major 3rd and resolves to the b7 (Bb) note.

Example 2n is a simple three-note-per-string ascending run. To make it less monotonous I've included a few hammer-ons and pull-offs to vary the timing. I've also included a bend from an "outside" note (because that's what cool people do).

Stylistically, it's reminiscent of Mark Tremonti and Slash. I've seen both players use this little trick over diatonic runs to make them more interesting and less linear. You can, of course, apply this approach to any mode using its three-note-per-string scale shape.

Example 2n: Tremonti-style G Dorian three-note-per-string ascending lick

This next idea uses G Minor pentatonic with an added "blue" grace note and a run that descends diatonically through G Dorian.

Example 2o: G Minor pentatonic with blue grace note and major 6th

Joining pentatonic and diatonic scales together is always refreshing to hear. It has melodic impact because the pentatonic scale has no semitone intervals, yet the diatonic scale does. This means you can quickly jump from a rocky-blues sound to something more heart-warming, emotional and bittersweet. Be wary when playing passages like this that you resolve to a note that complements the backing chords. Choose a specific note e.g. ending the run on a Bb over a Gm7 chord to highlight the minor 3rd.

Example 2p combines a basic G Minor triad arpeggio with descending diatonic notes from the Dorian scale.

Example 2p: Five-string G Minor arpeggio with G Dorian diatonic descent

Licks like this can be executed as a slow arpeggio or a quick sweep – it's completely up to you and will depend on your taste and what you think fits the song, composition or solo. I've heard Alexi Laiho from Children of Bodom use licks like this to make his entry into a fast, long descending run more triumphant. You will also notice that I've added slides to make the phrase more interesting and give it some flair. This also forces you to shift to a different section of the neck.

This next lick is based around a Gm7 arpeggio with an added E note to get more of the Dorian major 6th flavour.

Example 2q: Gm7 arpeggio with added major 6th

You can mess around with various expressive techniques to make arpeggios (and scales) sound less mechanical. In this instance I used slides, legato and a cheeky bend to give the phrase more feeling and add a fleeting moment of sexy blues.

The next lick features a concept I touched on earlier that I use all the time in Dorian soloing. When playing in G Dorian, the i chord (Gm) can be used as a substitute for the vi chord (Em7b5). Therefore, the reverse is true: the vi chord can substitute for the i chord. Example 2r uses the notes of Em7b5 (E G Bb D) over a G Minor chord. The note order has been rearranged to make the lick less boring and linear sounding.

Example 2r: Em7b5 arpeggio 1 3 2 4 3 5 lick

Notice that the notes used in the previous example are essentially a Gm triad (G Bb D) with an E note at the front. Once again we're highlighting that delicious Dorian note. For a great example of this, listen to Marty Friedman's solo on *Symphony of Destruction* by Megadeth. He plays an F#m7b5 arpeggio (ii chord in the key of E Minor) over the A Minor backing chord (chord iv in E Minor). It's well supported by the music and sounds more interesting than straight ascending and descending arpeggio triads.

The next example uses another Em7b5 arpeggio, but rearranges the order of the notes to make a simple, cool movable shape you can use across three octaves. It also uses a few mini-arpeggio triads in the descending part of the lick.

Example 2s: Crawling three octave Em7b5 arpeggio lick with descending mini arpeggios

In the next lick we'll be using position four of the G Minor pentatonic scale in an ascending manner with legato five-note groupings. The lick resolves with a descending Gm7 arpeggio with an added major 6th, once again hammering home that Dorian sound.

Example 2t: G Minor pentatonic position four with five-note legato groupings and Gm7 descending arpeggio

As you can see, the lick ends with a bend from a Db note. This is not from the G Dorian scale but is, however, the b5 of G. If we bend it up a semitone, the effect is to change a tense, outside note into a pleasant "in key" note. In this instance I've bent the Db to a D note, the fifth of G.

Example 2u takes a simple G Minor pentatonic shape in the first position with the addition of the major 6th and some tapped notes. The tapped notes suggest G Minor pentatonic in the second position. The fretting hand will occasionally highlight the E note for a more characteristically Dorian sound.

Example 2u: G Minor pentatonic with major 6th and tapped notes

This last lick is easily the silliest and most terrifying. We're going to combine an ascending Per Nilsson style Gm11 arpeggio with a descending Em7b5 arpeggio. This lick also includes a few outside notes, borrowed from the three-note-per-string Lydian diatonic scale shape, but we won't worry about that now!

Example 2v: Gm11 into Em7b5 arpeggio lick with ascending Dorian diatonic notes

Again, a lick like this forces you to make a position shift. It's a cool way of covering a large distance on the neck and is especially helpful if you have a tendency to get trapped in box positions. You may just like the feeling of longer, more horizontal passages. #whateverfloatsyourboat

Every lick we've learnt in this chapter can be transferred to other keys. Find some jam tracks or Dorian songs to play along to and try out these ideas. The more you play and listen, the more you'll uncover that bittersweet Dorian emotion that has been dying to come out of you.

Chapter 3: Phabulous Phrygian

Since the dark ages, a melodic evil, a mode of great power, has lived at the centre of the earth. It has been foretold in stories of folklore, superstition and urban legend that this mode is the last thing you hear before … being chased and eaten by a shark. Of course, I'm referring to the Phrygian mode.

Phrygian is the third of the seven diatonic modes. It's signature tense, foreboding sound has been used in everything from flamenco to thrash metal and, indeed, any other sub-genres seeking to attain a satanic sounding edge.

Part 1: Finding the Phrygian sound

In this chapter, the B Phrygian mode will be used for all our examples. Let's start by looking at a B Phrygian scale in one octave.

Example 3a:

As always, we should learn every mode as an individual scale in its own right, but it doesn't hurt to bear a few things in mind. B Phrygian can be viewed in a couple of ways:

1. As the third mode of G Major.

2. As a B Aeolian (Natural Minor) scale with a b2.

It's easy to see this if we compare B Aeolian and B Phrygian side by side.

B Aeolian = B **C#** D E F# G A

B Phrygian = B **C** D E F# G A B

Example 3b:

Aeolian scale formula = 1 2 b3 4 5 b6 b7

Phrygian scale formula = 1 b2 b3 4 5 b6 b7

The only difference between the two modes is the second note. The Aeolian mode has a full tone between root and second (B to C#). The Phrygian has just a semitone (B to C), which creates a very tense sound. Just as the major 6th was the "character" note of the Dorian mode, the b2 provides the Phrygian's signature evil sound.

Thinking of the Phrygian mode as "a minor scale with a b2" might seem like enough to get a theoretical understanding of the mode's sound, but the best way to hear a mode's characteristic sound is in context, with a chord progression.

We can hear the Phrygian's characteristic b2 interval by playing it over the simple chord progression shown below. Play through the power-chord progression, then play through the descending and ascending version of the scale.

Try this over the Phrygian backing track too!

Example 3c: B Phrygian chord progression with scale descend & ascend

The b2 is an outright tense interval, as it forms a semitone clash with the tonic home note (B). We can hear this in the interplay between the B5 and C5 chord. The C note from the B Phrygian scale is obviously present in the C5 chord, and you can the Phrygian mode's characteristic b2 in both the power-chords and the descending and ascending scale runs immediately after.

It's no wonder that the Phrygian is the go-to mode for thrash metal, nu-metal and for conjuring up tension in film scores. Who could forget the shark attack scenes in the *Jaws* films? Possibly the best and most effective use of the Phrygian mode EVER! It's abrasive, dark quality also makes it the perfect mode for adding drama and intensity to flamenco music.

To further familiarise yourself with the Phrygian mode's characteristic sound, have a listen to these Phrygian-based songs:

- Symphony of Destruction – Megadeth

- Wherever I May Roam – Metallica

- Over the Wall – Testament

- She Wants To Move – N.E.R.D.

- White Rabbit – Jefferson Airplane

Part 2: The Phrygian diatonic chords

In the case of the Phrygian, the semitone relationship between the i and the bII chords creates the most poignant tension and produces its signature sound. Let's take a look at the diatonic chords of the Phrygian mode compared to the Ionian.

Diatonic chords built from Ionian

maj	min	min	maj	maj	min	min7b5 (or 1/2 diminished)
I	ii	iii	IV	V	vi	vii

Diatonic chords built from Phrygian

min	maj	maj	min	min7b5	maj	min
i	bII	bIII	iv	v	bVI	bvii

Example 3d:

39

i   bII   bIII   iv   v   bVI   bvii

Bm   C   D   Em   F#m7(b5)   G   Am

When composing using a mode, we want to pick chords that reflect its distinct character and feeling. In the case of the Phrygian, we'll want to highlight the minor 2nd (b2). The easiest way to do this is to play any chord that contains the b2 flavour note. In B Phrygian, the b2 flavour note is C.

C Major (bII chord) = C E G

A Minor (bvii chord) = A C E

F#m7b5 (v chord) = F# A C E

Try writing a few progressions using these chords, preferably beginning and ending on B Minor. Here are two ideas to get you started:

Example 3e – Progression 1:

Bm   C   D   Am

Example 3f – Progression 2:

Bm   Em   D   C

Part 3: Soloing in Phrygian using scales and arpeggios

I've said this 1,000 times, but it's often hard to know where to start when soloing modally! As usual, I ask myself these questions:

1. What is a three-note-per-string version of the scale from the root?

2. What kind of pentatonics can I use e.g. regular, custom or relative minor?

3. What kinds of arpeggios will bring out the flavour of the mode?

Let's take the diatonic B Phrygian scale and stretch it across six strings with a three-note-per-string pattern.

Example 3g:

This is a good scale shape to begin with if you're new to the Phrygian sound. Highlighting the minor 3rd (D) evokes the melancholy sound of the minor scale, but the b2 (C) is the most flavoursome note and the one I always try to emphasise.

Pentatonics

We know that the versatile minor pentatonic scale can work for all of the minor modes – Aeolian, Dorian and Phrygian. It uses the 1st, 3rd, 4th, 5th and 7th intervals only – thus omitting the b2. Here is a regular descending B Minor pentatonic pattern, and the same pattern with added b2.

Example 3h:

Let's look at the remaining four positions of B Minor pentatonic, comparing the regular scale and the scale with added b2, side by side.

Example 3i:

Remember that you can choose to add in the b2, or not, and switch between the two highlighting the Phrygian sound as appropriate.

Arpeggios

Lastly, let's look at how to *Phrygianize* (a term I just coined) our arpeggios. By this I mean to take a simple B Minor arpeggio and add in the b2 (C) to add modal flavour. Compare the two arpeggios below.

Example 3j:

Here is another common five-string minor arpeggio shape, and the same arpeggio with an added b2.

Example 3k:

Finally, this Bm7 arpeggio covers all six strings in a diagonal, crawling manner spanning three octaves. Here it is without, and with, the b2.

Example 3l:

All of these arpeggios are useful for Phrygian soloing and it's good to have options, but they can also be used over a iii chord in any progression or key. You can be subtle and stay with the straight minor, or highlight the more evil Phrygian sound in your playing. All these ideas will work extremely well in death metal, thrash metal and sassy flamenco.

Part 4: Phrygian licks to help you get creative

To avoid giving you a bunch of scales and arpeggio shapes and not showing you how to use them properly, I've prepared some licks to bring all these melodic ideas together in an expressive, musical context.

The first lick we'll look at uses a classic a Chuck Berry pentatonic lick in B Minor, but I've added a C note to introduce the Phrygian b2 sound.

The classic bluesy pentatonic approach with bends is a familiar sound, but the hammer-ons and pull-offs between the B and C notes on the first string create the semitone tension crucial to the Phrygian sound.

Example 3m: B Minor pentatonic Chuck Berry lick with b2 legato notes.

Example 3n uses another custom Phrygian pentatonic that spans multiple octaves. The notes used can also be viewed as the exotic E Hirajoshi scale (E F# G B C). To make the lick more interesting, it crawls in an ascending, diagonal manner that forces multiple position shifts over three octaves. This is much more interesting than a standard two-note-per-string vertical pentatonic box. I've also added a few hammer-ons for smoothness and pace.

Example 3n: Crawling E Hirajoshi with five-note groupings

I wasn't too creative with the order of the notes in this lick, but you can use it to create a shreddy build up to another lick. The main thing is that I've planted the seed of an idea for you to go away and be creative with!

This next idea uses a three-note-per-string B Phrygian scale shape across six strings. I'm using triplet shreds with the occasional cheeky moment of legato to keep things interesting. It's reminiscent of Trivium and Racer X. It's easy to fall into a monotonous pattern with three-note-per-string shapes, so mess around with different legato note placement and timing.

Example 3o: Racer X style B Phrygian building shred lick

The next lick combines a simple five-string B Minor triad arpeggio with descending notes from the B Phrygian mode. The descending pattern suggests F# Locrian and I have used quavered triplets to add a bit of a swinging bounce to the lick.

Example 3p: Five-string B Minor arpeggio with F# Locrian three-note-per-string descent

Combining arpeggios and diatonic runs adds interest to an otherwise straightforward descending lick. It means we can jump from the wider intervals of an arpeggio to the closer intervals of a scale. You can apply this idea to any mode and explore it using three-, four- and six-string arpeggios.

Example 3q uses a B pedal note. I tried to keep this lick mainly to one string as I've seen Kirk Hammett and Michael Paget (Bullet For My Valentine) do a similar thing in solos and it's always sounded cool to me. Pedal notes really help to build tension. As the Phrygian is already a tense sounding mode, adding in the pedalling technique makes it an unstoppable force… for evil! Experiment with adding a pedal note on a few different strings and see what you can come up with.

Example 3q: Pedal B Phrygian lick

In the next example I thought it would be fun to give you a crazy arpeggio across all six strings using the 1st, 3rd, 5th, 7th, b9th (the b2 up an octave) and 11th intervals of the B Phrygian mode.

This would be a great way to start a solo or a cheeky lick for improvisation. It ticks all those nasty, tense Phrygian boxes. Be careful not to overuse an idea like this. Instead, think of it as a secret weapon for special occasions – like a bazooka loaded with Honey Badgers, or sword made entirely from liquorice (yes, I have just revealed my Kryptonite!)

Example 3r: Bm11(b9) sliding arpeggio lick

Here is an idea based on the B Phrygian three-note-per-string shape, which combines a few different techniques. It has fast triplet 1/16th notes played using rolling legato, with the addition of taps and strings skips.

Example 3s: B Phrygian three-note-per-string skipped legato lick with taps

Using rolling legato and taps is a great way to create speed without shredding or sweeping. The string skips create interesting intervallic jumps mid-lick, to provide the listener with some melodic curve balls to keep them intrigued.

Example 3t uses a B Minor pentatonic shape with an added b2. One thing that's interesting about this lick is the inconsistency of the number of notes on each string. Three-note-per-string patterns can cause us to fall into the trap of predictable triplet runs or robotic shred. Using a pattern like this encourages us to think in a less formulaic, mathematical manner and forces much less predictable lines.

Example 3t: B Minor pentatonic with b2 legato lick

The next lick uses a classic rock descending B Minor triplet pattern, then shifts into an ascending scale run using a segment of the A Dorian three-note-per-string shape. We can use A Dorian in a B Phrygian context as both modes come from the same key of G Major, thus they share the same notes.

Example 3u: B Minor pentatonic descending triplet lick with A Dorian three-note-per-string ascent

Our final lick uses another pedal idea with the open B string. It has a somewhat ACDC *Thunderstruck* vibe to it. John Petrucci and Alexi Laiho have used this kind of lick in many of their solos. You won't always have the option to use open strings in your licks, so if the opportunity presents itself, *go for it!*

Example 3v: Pedal on open B string lick

The main consideration with open string licks is just to make sure the fretted notes are derived from the scale. Example 3v is ideally to be used over a B Phrygian chord progression. The fretted note choices would be any combination of C, D, E, F#, G and A to remain in key.

As with all the modes, finding an appropriate jam track to practise to is essential. With any luck you'll summon the thrashy, flamenco beast-yeti-monster that has always lived within your soul and has been itching to come out!

Chapter 4: Luscious Lydian

The next stop on our modal journey plunges us into a misty void; a mysterious, galactic space kingdom known as *Lydian*. Allow me to set the scene that the Lydian mode is so well known for.

Imagine yourself travelling at the speed of light through multiple galaxies, or flying majestically through the air like that kid and the weird dragon dog from *The Never Ending Story* (his name is Falkor, I just Googled it). Imagine yourself casually opening a mysterious treasure chest. Mist flows out and reveals a golden sword, covered in flames. It can achieve many mighty purposes including making the perfect soufflé and has the ability to cure the common head cold.

Now imagine that you have to sit down and compose a soundtrack for all these zany adventures. It must capture feelings of excitement, mystery, uncertainty and surrealism. You feelin' me? Because if you are, we are ready for our Lydian musical adventure to begin.

The Lydian is the fourth of our seven modes and is a major mode, which means it has a generally happy sound. However, it has a raised (or *sharp*) fourth degree. Its #4 is its character note – the note that has been used in countless Sci-Fi and Fantasy film scores. In fact, it is identical to the Ionian mode except for that one note. It has also been used to great effect in many compositions by guitar virtuosos such as Steve Vai, Joe Satriani and John Petrucci. The Lydian mode has even been known to make the occasional appearance in progressive rock/metal.

Part 1: Finding the Lydian sound

In this chapter we will be using C Lydian for all our examples. Let's start by playing the C Lydian scale in one octave.

Example 4a:

We can think of C Lydian in two ways. Again (and I know you're getting bored of this now) it's important to learn the Lydian mode as an individual scale, but it doesn't hurt to know a few of its pseudonyms. Lydian is…

1. The fourth mode of the major scale

2. Identical to the major scale except for its #4 note

Let's compare C Ionian and C Lydian side by side:

C Ionian (C D E **F** G A B C)

C Lydian (C D E **F#** G A B C)

Example 4b:

Ionian scale formula = 1 2 3 4 5 6 7

Lydian scale formula = 1 2 3 #4 5 6 7

As you can see, the only difference between the two scales is the fourth note. The Ionian mode has a semitone interval between the third and fourth notes, while the Lydian has a full tone, creating the raised 4th (#4).

The #4 is the most important note in the scale and what gives the Lydian its spacey, dreamlike and somewhat uplifting, characteristic sound.

Comparing the two scales mentioned above gives you a quick overview of the Lydian mode's intervals and differentiating characteristic note. However, having the knowledge that Lydian is essentially a "major scale with a #4" means very little if we have no understanding of how the scale works in context over chord progressions.

Let's look at a simple chord progression using characteristically Lydian sounding chords. We'll play two bars of chords and two bars of simple scale runs that ascend and descend. This will help you get used to not only the sound of the scale, but the chords that create the overall mood as well.

Play the following example and try the scale ideas over the Lydian backing track.

Example 4c: C Lydian chord progression with scale ascend & descend

Scale Runs

The #4 (F#) note is the characteristic note of C Lydian and is included in the Cmaj7(#11) and D7 chords. When we combine the scale with these chords, we have a fuller understanding of the Lydian sound.

With these elements in mind, we can use the Lydian mode to create moments of drama, tension and galactic adventure in songs. It is often used as a compositional tool to create a tense dramatic bridge or outro to a song.

Lydian is used repeatedly in film scores. Picture a spaceship landing. The mystery and tension build as the doors slowly open, then … BAM! Out pops an alien. Or, if you're watching Jodie Foster in the 1997 Sci-Fi blockbuster *Contact,* a blurry, possibly alien or monster-like figure in the distance… and it turns out it's her dad. (Cough, cough... insert rolling tumbleweed here).

Here are some examples of Lydian songs to get you used to its characteristic sound. See if you can add some Lydian songs to the list:

• Curve – John Petrucci

• Flying in a Blue Dream – Joe Satriani

• The Simpsons Theme – Danny Elfman

• Dreams – Fleetwood Mac

• E.T. The Extra-Terrestrial OST Far From Home – John Williams

Part 2: The Lydian diatonic chords

In the Lydian mode, there is a strong relationship between chord I and chord II. Having two major chords adjacent to one another contributes to this mode's happy sound, but also creates an unusual tension. Let's look at the diatonic chords of the Lydian, compared to the Ionian.

Diatonic chords starting from chord 1 (Ionian)

maj	min	min	maj	maj	min	min7b5 (or 1/2 diminished)
I	ii	iii	IV	V	vi	vii

Diatonic chords starting from chord four (Lydian)

maj	maj	min	min7b5	maj	min	min
I	II	iii	#iv	V	vi	vii

We can now take the notes of C Lydian (C D E F# G A B) and use them to create chords that relate to the mode.

Example 4d:

If we are composing with this mode, we'll want to include the chords that particularly highlight its "flavour" note – in the case of C Lydian, the F#. One easy approach is to create a progression that combines the IV and V chords, as there is no other example in a diatonic chord progression where two major chords appear, side by side, a whole tone apart. Other good choices are the vii or #iv chords.

Each of the chords below contain the characteristic F# note:

D Major (II chord) = D F# A

B Minor (vii chord) = B D F#

F#m7b5 (#iv chord) = F# A C E

Try writing a few chord progressions that use these chords, beginning and ending on a C Major chord, and get a feel for the Lydian sound. Here are two examples:

Example 4e – Progression 1:

Example 4f – Progression 2:

Part 3: Soloing in Lydian using scales and arpeggios

You've heard it thrice! … Now you're going to hear it a fourth time!

1. What is a three-note-per-string version of the scale from the root?

2. What kind of pentatonics can I use e.g. regular, custom or relative minor?

3. What kinds of arpeggios will bring out the flavour of the mode?

Here is the diatonic Lydian scale across all six strings, using a three-note-per-string pattern.

Example 4g:

When playing the Lydian mode, I'll always highlight the major 3rd (E in C Lydian) to conjure up that major sound, but the raised 4th (F#) is the tense flavour note, so I insist on emphasising this too. It's what gives the mode its quirky, spacey sound. If you highlight Lydian's major 7th (B) it can create the sound of a "hanging note" and adds further tension.

Pentatonics

In the case of the Lydian mode, a cool substitution idea is to play a minor pentatonic scale four semitones up from the root. Instead of the C Lydian scale we can therefore play E Minor pentatonic.

Example 4h:

You can also use all the other minor pentatonic box shapes and sneak in a blue note – the b5 of E (Bb).

The E Hirajoshi scale I mentioned in the previous chapter also works really well in place of C Lydian, the notes of which are E, F#, G, B and C (1 2 b3 5 b6).

Example 4i:

Not only does this scale summon ninjas, it has a nice creepy, tense vibe due to its emphasis of the minor 6th. The reason this scale works so well in a C Lydian context is that it also highlights the major 3rd and major 7th notes of C Lydian – both of which are important to its character. If you begin the E Hirajoshi scale on a C note instead of an E, you end up with what I like to call a "Lydian pentatonic box", which is made up of the notes C E F# G and B.

Let's look at C Minor pentatonic and "C Lydian pentatonic" side by side:

Example 4j:

If ninjas played lead guitar, this would surely be the kind of scale they'd play soon after avenging their grandfather's death at the hands of the neighbouring rival ninja clan. In the context of C Lydian there will be five, two-note-per-string E Hirajoshi scales shapes across the fretboard.

Example 4k:

Arpeggios

Let's talk arpeggios. The standard major triad is made up of the 1st, 3rd and 5th notes of a major scale (C, E and G in C Major). To bring out the Lydian flavour we'll add in the raised 4th (F#).

The arpeggio below uses a high register and spans two octaves using the most common five-string shape, with the addition of the #4. Let's compare a standard C Major triad with its *Lydianised* variation.

Example 4l:

The next arpeggio uses a slightly less common five-string shape, played in a lower register.

Example 4m:

When used over a I chord, or a droning C Lydian riff, these scale shapes and arpeggios are a great way to bring out the poignant characteristics of this mode. You can also use them in any mode or chord progression when the right chord change presents itself! For example, you could use a *Lydianised* arpeggio over a IV chord in an Ionian progression, or a III chord in a Dorian progression, etc.

Part 4: Lydian licks to help you get creative

Now it's time to see how these melodic ideas can be used in a musical context. Example 4n is a three-note-per-string diatonic run I use quite a lot when improvising. This idea can be applied to any mode, but I am particularly fond of using it in a Lydian context.

Notice that I've added in a few hammer-ons and pull-offs to make it less robotic and linear. I've also included two triplets to break up the straight 1/16th note pattern. There are a few moments where the lick descends briefly, to stop it sounding like an ascending scale.

Experiment with changing the placement of legato notes and triplets. Be creative and mess around with this until you find a combination of notes that sound the way you like.

Example 4n: Tremonti-style C Lydian ascending lick

The next example uses the substitute mentioned earlier, E Minor Pentatonic (E, G, A, B and D) which nicely captures the Lydian sound, but in this instance I've added in the missing diatonic notes (C and F#) every so often to add to the flavour.

Example 4o: E Minor Pentatonic with C Lydian diatonic descent

We know from previous examples that the pentatonic has a great bluesy sound that works 99% of the time, but in a Lydian context its lack of semitones is conspicuous. We need that spacey note to create the dreamy Lydian sound, so we'll add in the #4 (F#). The addition of a B note creates an unresolved quality that fits perfectly with the Lydian vibe.

This next lick uses a C Major triad arpeggio with an added #4. This instantly gives us the Lydian sound and I've added some interesting position shifts, as well as a few 5th intervals to add to the futuristic, spacey sound.

Example 4p: Five-string C Major arpeggio plus #4 with descending slide lick

Example 4q uses a pedal C root note and gradually moves through the C Lydian scale. I've heard bands like Testament, Trivium and Judas Priest use licks like this in solos, often as a means of slowing things down and creating tension before a faster, more explosive passage, such as an epic shred or sweep picked arpeggio. Experiment by trying different pedal notes. You could try flipping this idea around and using a high note as the pedal tone while you descend down the scale.

Example 4q: C Lydian pedal lick

This next idea uses a major 7th arpeggio with a #4 spanning three octaves. I've also included some slides and a string skipped major 7th arpeggio that resolves to a sus2-shaped arpeggio.

Example 4r: Crawling diagonal E Hirajoshi lick with Cmaj7 string skip arpeggio descent

The major 7th interval is a feature of the Ionian mode too, so it's not a "Lydian only" sound, but when paired with the Lydian #4 you get two moments of lovely unresolved tension. This, of course, brings out the weird spacey vibe of Lydian and is a go-to staple for me – especially if I'm running out of material when improvising!

Example 4s uses the Lydian pentatonic (AKA Hirajoshi) idea we looked at earlier and is one of my favourite scale shapes. This example includes hammer-ons, slides, taps, bends and five-note groupings – all designed to make the timing of the phrase less predictable.

Example 4s: C Lydian pentatonic with ascending fives legato lick and taps

Five- and seven-note groupings are a really simple way to escape predictable four, eight and sixteen note patterns. They bring an element of surprise, as the emphasis falls on unexpected beats in the bar. This kind of lick can be used on any pentatonic or two-note-per-string scale, so mess around with it in a few different keys and modes.

The next lick opens with a combination of a Csus2 shape and an E Minor triad, the effect of which is somewhat like a Cmaj9 arpeggio. The lick drifts into an ascending E Hirajoshi run, then transitions into the E Minor Pentatonic scale.

I love this lick as it's incredibly diverse. Ninth arpeggios are far less used than triads or seventh arpeggios, so it instantly gives a fresher sound. The combination of the Hirajoshi and minor pentatonic scales produces a Japanese sounding hybrid blended with traditional blues.

Combining multiple scale flavours like this makes it hard for your licks to sound like they've been borrowed (stolen) from another player. We've all heard that one guy who *only* listens to SRV and Hendrix, whose licks sound like a stale, grating tribute. So at all costs, don't be that guy. *Never* be that guy!

Example 4t: Csus2/Cmaj9 arpeggio lick with E Hirajoshi run and slide into E Minor pentatonic

The next example uses the C Lydian three-note-per-string scale shape, but calls for a rolling legato technique as well as tapping. I've also added some string skips to create interesting intervallic jumps!

Remember that you can use this concept with any three-note-per-string mode shape. When adding tapped notes, make sure they are diatonic notes from the parent key. If you're feeling particularly daring, try this concept with the harmonic minor and other exotic scale shapes.

Example 4u: C Lydian three-note-per-string, string skip legato lick with taps

Example 4v utilises the E Hirajoshi scale again. The lick is fairly straightforward as it uses straight 1/16th notes with legato technique here and there to keep the phrasing loose and avoid sounding too robotic.

Example 4v: E Hirajoshi lick with hammer-ons and pull-offs

Don't hesitate to try this idea with other two-note-per-string scale shapes. Be brave, be daring and see what kind of licks you can come up with.

The final lick in this chapter combines a Cmaj7 arpeggio over six strings with the fifth position of the E Hirajoshi scale. This will sound characteristically Lydian. It also has a brief legato descending pattern working in groups of five, which if you haven't noticed, I'm obsessed with!

This lick is very ZOUPAFIED. I love six-string arpeggios with legato and slides; I love five note groupings; and I love resolving phrases that use bends going from outside to inside! That said, it's important when creating your own licks and solos that you gravitate towards what *you* love. This will help you cement your unique playing style and find your voice as a guitar player.

Example 4w: Six-string Cmaj7 arpeggio lick with Hirajoshi descending five and outside bend

In summary, everything you've learnt here can be moved to other Lydian keys. Find some Lydian jam tracks and play along until you find that spacey, tense, dreamy and sometimes groovy sound.

Chapter 5: The Magic of Mixolydian

In all my years studying music, the Mixolydian has been the standout mode that has fascinated me the most. My fascination stems from its incredible eclecticism and versatility. This can be seen through the mode's broad usage across multiple cultures, periods of time and musical genres.

If there was a planet called Mixolydian it would be inhabited by happy, jigging hobbits and skipping leprechauns. The streets would run rampant with charming parades, filled with painted Indian elephants and everyone would be listening to good time 80s glam metal. Furthermore, if they had floats in such parades, there would be a Steve Vai float, but he would only be allowed to play his guitar using the "mystical sitar" effect. As you can see, Mixolydian would be a mystical and charming world.

Mixolydian is the fifth of our seven diatonic modes. Known for its fist-raising sound and bounding positivity, it's no wonder this mode was used repeatedly throughout the 80s to create rock 'n' roll and glam metal anthems. It is also used frequently in traditional Celtic and Indian music. It was even used in medieval music! (Ask Sven from Skyrim. I apologise if that gag/reference is too obscure!)

Part 1: Finding the Mixolydian sound

In this chapter we will use E Mixolydian for all our examples. Let's start by playing the E Mixolydian scale in one octave.

Example 5a:

As well as being a scale and sound in its own right, we can think of Mixolydian in two other ways:

1. As the fifth mode of the parent major scale (in this case, E Mixolydian is the fifth mode of A Major).

2. As a major scale with a b7.

It's easy to spot what makes the Mixolydian distinct by comparing E Ionian and E Mixolydian side by side.

E Ionian = E F# G# A B C# **D#** E

E Mixolydian = E F# G# A B C# **D** E

Example 5b:

Ionian scale formula = 1 2 3 4 5 6 7

Mixolydian scale formula = 1 2 3 4 5 6 b7

The only difference between the two modes is the seventh note. The Ionian mode has a semitone interval between the 7th and the octave, whereas the Mixolydian has a full tone, which creates a b7 (b7 or dominant 7th) relationship with the root note.

This b7 note gives the Mixolydian mode its signature rock 'n' roll, dark blues and anthemic sounds, whereas the regular major 7th note of the Ionian has an unresolved, peaceful, yet contemplative sound. Even though only one note has been changed from Ionian to create the Mixolydian, the difference in sound and feeling is quite substantial.

As I've stated in previous chapters, comparing one scale to another will give you an understanding of intervals and the different scale formulas, but it will not increase your understanding of how the mode works in a musical context. The best way to achieve this is to hear the mode accompanied by chords.

Have a play through the example below. It's simple chord progression made up of four chords, followed by ascending and descending version of the E Mixolydian scale in one octave.

Example 5c: E Mixolydian chord progression with scale ascend & descend

The chord progression consists of E Major, D Major and A Major, which means the progression is made entirely of major chords. Stylistically, this is very common in Mixolydian rock progressions and compositions.

Side note: did you notice the progression above included the chord D Major? It's built on the b7 of the scale (the only difference between major and Mixolydian is that b7 note) so it's a great chord to use when outlining Mixolydian. You'll often see the tonic chord, in this case E Major, followed by a major chord one tone below (in this case D Major) in Mixolydian progressions. An excellent example of this change between the D and C chord occurs in *Sweet Child O' Mine*.

When the chord progression and scale are played after one another, you'll get that sense of a happy, yet kick-ass rock sound. With these factors in mind, it's easy to see why the Mixolydian mode is such an important staple of 80s party rock, glam metal and stadium rock music.

Here are some examples of Mixolydian songs:

- Nothing But A Good Time – Poison
- Glasgow Kiss – John Petrucci
- Royals – Lorde
- Sweet Child O' Mine – Guns N' Roses
- Highway To Hell – ACDC

Part 2: The Mixolydian diatonic chords

The distinct character of the Mixolydian mode comes from the relationship between the I and IV chords, and often the I and bVII chords. The important thing to note is that all three of these chords are major.

Let's compare the diatonic chords of the Ionian and Mixolydian modes:

Diatonic chords of Ionian

maj	min	min	maj	maj	min	min7b5 (or 1/2 diminished)
I	ii	iii	IV	V	vi	vii

Diatonic chords in Mixolydian

maj	min	min7b5		maj	min	min	maj
I	ii	iii		IV	v	vi	bVII

Example 5d:

When composing with the Mixolydian mode we normally want to highlight the b7. The easiest way is to pair the I chord in a progression with the bVII chord (the most fist-raising rock chord when it follows the V). Or we can highlight the v or iii chords. All of them contain the characteristic b7 (D).

D Major (chord bVII) = D F# A

B Minor (chord v) = B D F#

G#m7b5 (chord iii) = G# B D F#

Try writing a few chord progressions using these options, preferably starting and ending on E Major to capture the Mixolydian feel. Here are a couple of ideas:

Example 5e – Progression 1:

67

Example 5f – Progression 2:

E   D   Bm   D

```
T|--0--------------|--2--------------|--2--------------|--2--------------|
A|--0--------------|--3--------------|--3--------------|--3--------------|
 |--1--------------|--2--------------|--4--------------|--2--------------|
B|--2--------------|--0--------------|--4--------------|--0--------------|
 |--2--------------|                 |--2--------------|                 |
 |--0--------------|                 |                 |                 |
```

Part 3: Soloing in Mixolydian using scales and arpeggios

Sorry if I sound like a broken record by now, but…

1. What is a three-note-per-string version of the scale from the root?

2. What kind of pentatonics can I use e.g. regular, custom or relative minor?

3. What kinds of arpeggios will bring out the flavour of the mode?

Here the is three-note-per-string pattern for the Mixolydian across all six strings:

Example 5g:

```
T|----------------------------------------------------14--16--17----|
A|------------------------------13--14--16---14--15--17-------------|
 |-------------------12--14--16------------------------------------|
B|-------12--14--16------------------------------------------------|
 |12--14--16-------------------------------------------------------|
```

When playing in Mixolydian I like to highlight the major 3rd (G# in the key of E Mixolydian) to convey its happy, positive aspect, and its b7 (D) which is its most flavoursome note. The b7 brings the bluesy-yet-rocky feel to the scale and accentuates the stadium rock sound (as well as the more Celtic hobbit-like sound).

Pentatonics

Let's talk about pentatonics. You may or may not have heard the term "relative minor scale" before, so let's do a quick explanation without boring you to tears. Relative keys are major and minor scales with the same key signatures. The relative minor scale of G Major is E Minor (you can always locate the relative minor by descending three semitones from the root of your major scale on guitar). Many players opt to do this so they can play in the comfortable box of the minor pentatonic. We can apply this same concept to the Mixolydian too. Descending three semitones from the root (E) we arrive at the C# Minor pentatonic.

Example 5h:

The sexiest notes to highlight when using this pentatonic scale shape are the E (the root of E Mixolydian), G# (the major 3rd) and B (the 5th). But you can also add in the blue note G (the b5), as an erotic, outside passing tone.

This next scale shape is my favourite way to solo over a Mixolydian chord progression (or a V chord in an Ionian context). I call it the "Mixolydian pentatonic" because it uses the 1st, 3rd, 4th, 5th and 7th note of the Mixolydian scale. Let's compare the E Minor Pentatonic (E, G, A, B and D) and the E Mixolydian pentatonic (E, G#, A, B and D) side by side.

Example 5i:

The only difference between the two scales is that E Minor Pentatonic has a minor 3rd interval, while E Mixolydian pentatonic has a major 3rd. Using this scale shape, we can highlight both the major 3rd and the b7, which gives the Mixolydian its bluesy yet fist-raising sound. Then we can transfer this idea to the other positions of the minor pentatonic, *Mixolydianizing* them in the process ... and yes, I just made that word up. Let's compare the scales using those remaining positions.

Example 5j:

Position 2 E Mixolydian Pentatonic

Position 3 E Mixolydian Pentatonic

mf

```
T----------------------------------4--5-----|----------------------------5--7--|
A------------------------3--5-------|----------------------------5--9--------|
----------------2--4---|------------------4--7---|
B------2--6--|------------------6--7---|
----2--5---|----------5--7---|
--4--5---|----5--7---|
```

Position 4 E Mixolydian Pentatonic

Position 5 E Mixolydian Pentatonic

```
T----------------------------------7--10-----|--------------------------------10--12-|
A------------------------9--10------|------------------------------10--12---------|
----------------7--9---|------------------9--13---|
----------7--11---|----------9--12---|
B------7--10--|----11--12---|
----7--10---|----10--12---|
--10--12---|
```

Arpeggios

Now let's talk about the sexiest musical term of them all: *arpeggios!* In the case of the Mixolydian, I only want to focus on dominant arpeggios. An E7 arpeggio is made up of the first note of the scale (E), the major 3rd (G#), 5th (B) and b7 (D). The D is our Mixolydian "flavour" note, so this arpeggio perfectly complements the Mixolydian sound. Let's look at three different ways to play an E7 arpeggio.

The first arpeggio uses the most common five-string major triad shape and adds the b7. Let's compare the basic triad and the dominant 7 arpeggio side by side.

Example 5k:

mf

```
T--------------------------4----7----|------------------------------4----7-|
A--------------------5-----|----------------------------5--------|
----------------4---|-------------------4----7---|
A----------6--|--------------6---|
B----7---|----5----7---|
--7---|--5---|
```

The next arpeggio is based on a less common five-string major triad shape. Once again, we'll look at the arpeggio as a regular triad and dominant 7 arpeggio side by side.

Example 5l:

The final shape is an E7 arpeggio spanning all six strings covering three and a bit octaves. Let's compare it to the straight triad again to hear the different flavour the dominant note brings to the arpeggio.

Example 5m:

Keep in mind that these arpeggio shapes are moveable into other Mixolydian keys. They are useable in any mode over diatonic and non-diatonic dominant chords!

Part 4: Mixolydian licks to help you get creative!

Here are some licks and concepts to get you using the Mixolydian mode in creative, musical way. In the first lick we'll use the Mixolydian pentatonic scale shape to create a 1/16th note lick with a five-note grouping pulse.

Example 5n: E Mixolydian pentatonic lick with descending fives

I like to use legato technique in five-note pulse licks to add speed and a fluent flurry of notes. The odd number pulse over an even 16th note passage means that the notes appear less "on the beat" and more unpredictable. If you get a taste for interesting patterns with odd pulses, this concept works with regular pentatonics too and also sounds interesting and less predictable if you use seven-note patterns.

Example 5o is based on the Mixolydian pentatonic, but I've changed the note order from the usual 1, 3, 4, 5, 7 pattern (E G# A B D) to 3, 4, 5, 7, 1, 7 (G# A B D E D E). This lick is more fun to play than your usual two-note-per-string pentatonic box shape. It crawls diagonally across the fretboard instead of vertically.

This lick is a cool way to cover a vast melodic range on the guitar, but also calls for position shifts at each octave. Notice the cool sound created by using a seven-note pattern with a triplet feel.

Example 5o: Crawling diagonal Mixolydian pentatonic lick

The next idea uses a simple three-note-per-string diatonic scale shape in E Mixolydian and adds a smooth legato technique with a seven-note pulse.

Example 5p: E Mixolydian rolling legato in sevens with cheeky outside bend

Rolling legato is a great way to create a different kind of speed to normal shred speed. Legato licks like this are particularly interesting because they juxtapose a smooth relaxed vibe with somehow sounding chaotic. I resolved the lick above by bending from an outside note to a scale note. It's a sound I've grown fond of due to growing up listening to and loving Marty Friedman and Cacophony! Bear in mind, this kind of legato playing can be used on any three-note-per-string scale shape.

Example 5q combines an E7 arpeggio with a diatonic descending scale pattern using straight 16th notes. I've included a slide to make the position shift more manageable and seamless.

Notice that the E7 arpeggio starts on a D note – the b7 of the arpeggio, highlighting the b7 Mixolydian sound. The arpeggio also slides into a D note before descending a relatively predictable scale pattern.

Keep in mind that arpeggios are like chord inversions. We don't have to start and finish on the root note. The most important thing to concern yourself with is the notes of the arpeggio. I'll often say to my students, "It's the sum of the parts, not the order of the notes that make the chord." Which is also true of arpeggios. Try mixing different arpeggio shapes with different diatonic scale descents. It will create more interesting intervals, as well as highlighting different aspects of the mode you're working with.

Example 5q: Five-string E7 arpeggio with slide into sixteenths descending pattern

This next lick combines the third position of the E Mixolydian Pentatonic with the second position of the C# Minor Pentatonic. I've added in some legato technique to add smoothness, as well as the occasional triplet and some slides to help with position shifts.

Bear in mind that each of these pentatonic scales brings something different to the table. E Mixolydian Pentatonic has a semitone interval (G# to A) which creates tension and wants to resolve. C# Minor Pentatonic has no semitones and is a bit more predictable, with a straight rocky-blues sound. Blending different sounding scales together is a great way to keep your licks and solos sounding fresh!

Example 5r: E Mixolydian Pentatonic legato lick with slide transition into C# Minor Pentatonic descent

Here is a lick that uses pedal notes from E Mixolydian to drift into a "meat and veg" C# Minor Pentatonic run. It builds slowly by ascending the notes of E Mixolydian, then the pedal note changes from an E to a G#. Then we bring it home with the semiquaver speed of the C# Minor Pentatonic lick.

Example 5s: Mid-register E Mixolydian pedal lick with slide into C# Minor Pentatonic

Try experimenting with changing timing mid-lick. Too many 1/16th notes or triplets in a row can become tiresome and predictable.

Example 5t is based on a six-string E7 arpeggio that uses hammer-ons and slides to make it sound less robotic. It transitions into C# Minor Pentatonic and highlights the "blue" b5 note (G) on the third string 12th fret. Using the relative minor scale like this is a great option, because it produces a happy-yet-bluesy sound that works perfectly over Mixolydian progressions.

Example 5t: Six-string E7 arpeggio lick with slide transition into C# Minor Pentatonic

Next, try this descending legato version of the E Mixolydian three-note-per-string shape. I've included a few taps to introduce an element of surprise along the way. The taps also make the legato rolls on each string last a bit longer.

Example 5u: E Mixolydian three-note-per-string legato lick with taps and slides

The next lick uses the open first string to create a droning E pedal note. Such opportunities aren't available in every key, so when they are, it's good to capitalise on them.

Example 5v: Open E string pedal ascending Mixolydian lick

```
T ---------4-5-4-0-5-7-5-0-7-9-7-0-9-10-9-0----12-10-0-----10-0-16-12-0----12-0-12 16 12----12----------------- full
A -------------------------------------------------------12----------------15--------------15-----15-------------
B ---------------------------------------------------------------------------------------------------------------
```

The final lick uses multiple positions of the A Major scale, which shares the same notes as E Mixolydian. It sneakily introduces fragments of G# Locrian, A Ionian and B Dorian three-note-per-string scale shapes. I started on a G# note because I wanted to highlight the third degree of E Mixolydian. The Locrian mode just happened to correspond with this particular note and key signature. This lick uses a relatively simple legato approach, but includes a few slides to create subtle position shifts.

Example 5w: G# Locrian three-note-per-string legato lick with sliding position shift

```
                                                          ½
T -----------------------------------------------9-------------
A --------------4-5-7-9-7-5---5-7-9-----6-7-9--6-7-9-11-9-7--7-9-11-
B ----4-5-7----------------9----------------11------------------
```

Go and seek out some Mixolydian jam tracks and jam along until you unlock the fist-raising, glam rock, Celtic beast you never knew existed inside you!

Chapter 6: Astonishing Aeolian

The Aeolian mode is the sixth of our seven diatonic modes and is more commonly known as the Natural Minor scale. The Aeolian is the most used of all the minor modes and can be heard in 99% of all the sad songs ever written.

The Aeolian is the most obviously sad and "minor sounding" of the modes. Most ballads and broken-hearted love songs use the Aeolian mode to create the melodies and chord progressions that tug at our heartstrings.

The one exception to the *Aeolian mode = sad song* rule is the use of the Ionian mode in the classic song *On Top of Spaghetti* – an unforgettable ballad about sneezing, and the mourning of a man who has recently become separated from his poor meatball.

The Aeolian is often referred to as the *relative minor* scale. The boring theory rule is that building a scale on the sixth degree of any major scale forms the relative minor, which functions as the "sad mommy" counterpart to the "happy daddy" major scale.

To find the relative minor of any major scale, you just need to count up six notes from the root of the major scale and start a new scale from there. For example, G Major's relative minor is E Minor and D Major's relative minor is B Minor etc.

Remember, modes contain exactly the same notes as their parent scale, so A Aeolian contains exactly the same notes as the C Major scale, but begins and ends on the note A. Beginning on the sixth note of the major scale creates a new pattern of tones that sound very different from pattern of notes in the major scale.

Check out the pattern of tones and semitones below, and compare the formulas of Aeolian and Ionian:

Aeolian: T St T T St T T (Formula 1 2 b3 4 5 b6 b7)

A Aeolian = A B C D E F G

Ionian T T St T T T St (Formula 1 2 3 4 5 6 7)

C Ionian = C D E F G A B C

You can immediately see from the b3 that the Aeolian is a minor mode.

When I think of the Aeolian mode I see a deep well of sadness. I think of every slow, emotional song Tori Amos and Evanescence have ever written. I think of an emo kid's poem, written on the back of a black and white photo of a tortured willow tree!

But the most Aeolian thing I can think of is the hypothetical situation where I have put bread in my toaster, only to realise there's no margarine in the house! As a result, I have a very difficult choice to make…

1. Eat the toast dry.

2. Feed it to the local gang of pigeon street toughs (who would most likely take it by force anyway).

Either way, I find myself overcome with a deep wave of sadness, loss and disappointment. I feel my eyes well up and hear the sound of violins in the distance. I run to the park near my childhood home with tears streaming down my face, thinking, "Why did this happen to me?!"

I run till I'm out of breath and collapse by a small playground. I am alone next to a creaky swing seat that hasn't been used in years. There was a time where you'd come to this park and find laughing children playing here every day. Now this once happy place is riddled with bird poop and graffitied obscenities. The grey skies rumble and, within a few short moments, I'm drenched in rain, mud swirling at my feet, as though Zeus himself has taken it upon himself to punish me. I can almost hear him bellowing from the highest peak of Mount Olympus,

"Nobody likes you!"

At this moment I am fully immersed in the emotive force that is the Aeolian mode. I think you get the picture…

Part 1: Finding the Aeolian sound

In this chapter we'll use the E Aeolian scale (AKA The E Natural Minor) for our examples. The notes in E Aeolian are E F# G A B C D

Let's play the E Aeolian scale in one octave.

Example 6a:

Scale intervals: T St T T St T W

Scale formula: 1 2 b3 4 5 b6 b7

Aeolian will probably sound familiar to you, as it's the most commonly used of the minor modes (modes that contain a b3). The b3, b6 and b7 are where this mode gets all its sadness from. When you turn on the radio and hear a sad song, it's probably because the Aeolian/Natural Minor scale was used to write the chord progression and an array of upsetting melodies.

As you've seen in earlier chapters, we use the "common" sounding Ionian and Aeolian mode formulas as a point of reference when we learn more daunting and interesting modes. Examining how other minor modes – such as the Dorian and Phrygian – are constructed compared to the Aeolian will help you identify the nuances and characteristics that make them different.

When we played through the Ionian mode in the first chapter, it was obvious that it was just the common, well-known major scale. As you play through the Aeolian, you may say, "Hey, hang on! Isn't this just the Natural Minor scale? Why, like the Ionian, does it have a weird/bogus name?"

It's important to identify the fact that we are using the Aeolian mode because the term "minor scale" is very broad and could refer to several scales (Dorian and Phrygian are minor scales, as are the Melodic, Harmonic and Hungarian minor scales). Being specific is incredibly important.

The standout characteristics of the Aeolian mode are its natural 2nd and b6th – in the case of E Aeolian, F# and C respectively. The combination of these two intervals are what separates the Aeolian from the Dorian and Phrygian modes.

We can hear these characteristic notes and their functions more clearly in the simple chord progression in the diagram below. Play through the four-chord progression and then play the ascending and descending variations of the one octave Aeolian scale.

Example 6b: E Aeolian chord progression w/scale ascend & descend

We can hear the natural 2nd (F#) note in the VII (D Major chord), and the b6th (C) note is present in the bVI (C Major chord). The overall sound of the chords and scale together is the characteristically sombre sound that makes the Aeolian mode the first point of call for composing songs about break-ups, loss and especially mourning. It is used frequently in film and television scores to emphasise moments of sadness and trauma.

As you continue to build your knowledge of theory and scales, and grow more confident in your mastery of the fretboard, it's important to remember that nothing compares to having a sound and feeling with which to associate these modes. Here are some Aeolian-based songs to listen to. As previously, seek out and add other songs to the list.

• Save Tonight – Eagle Eye Cherry

• Nothing Else Matters – Metallica

• Polly – Nirvana

- Kryptonite – 3 Doors Down

- Zombie – The Cranberries

Part 2: The Aeolian diatonic chords

In every chapter of this book, I have underlined the importance of knowing the diatonic chords of a key or mode. This knowledge will help you to determine the colours and emotions you may wish to highlight. In the Aeolian mode the most important chord is the i – a minor chord – which is also the vi chord in Ionian progressions. It sets the scene for sad things to come and works particularly well when paired with the bVI or iv chord. The interplay between these three chords are crucial to convey Aeolian's signature melancholy sound.

Let's look at the diatonic chords of the Aeolian mode compared to the Ionian:

Diatonic chords in Ionian:

maj	min	min	maj	maj	min	min7b5 (or 1/2 diminished)
I	ii	iii	IV	V	vi	vii

Diatonic chords in Aeolian:

min	min7b5	maj	min	min	maj	maj
i	ii	bIII	iv	v	bVI	bVII

Now we can take the notes of the E Aeolian scale (E F# G A B C D) and use them to form the following chords.

Example 6c:

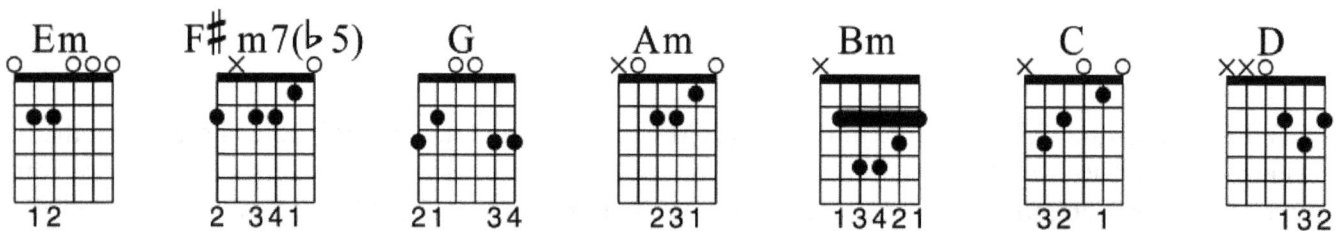

Like the Ionian mode, the characteristics of Aeolian are not as poignant as some other modes. But we can highlight the Aeolian sound and differentiate it from other modes by using chords that contain the b6. In the Aeolian, this interval is more helpless and sombre sounding than the Dorian's natural 6th. The Aeolian's major 2nd is also more subtle and less grating than the Phrygian's b2.

If we begin a progression with the tonic chord (Em), we could follow it with the bVI chord (C Major), as it obviously contains a C note (the b6). We could also use the v or ii chords, as both contain an F# (the Aeolian major 2nd).

C Major (bVI chord) = C E G

B Minor (v chord) = B D F#

F#m7b5 (ii chord) = F# A C E

Try writing a few chord progressions using these chords and try to begin and end on an E Minor chord to get a feel for the Aeolian chord progression. Here are a couple of quick ideas.

Example 6d – Progression 1:

Example 6e – Progression 2:

Part 3: Soloing in Aeolian using scales and arpeggios

I've mentioned this five times now! Let's put together a soloing checklist for Aeolian and ask ourselves the three big questions:

1. What is a three-note-per-string version of the scale from the root?

2. What kind of pentatonics can I use e.g. regular, custom or relative minor?

3. What kinds of arpeggios will bring out the flavour of the mode?

Here is the diatonic Aeolian scale spanning six strings with a three-note-per-string pattern.

Example 6f:

This is great way to hear the mode across the neck and an excellent tool for improvisation and composition.

Pentatonics

Next, I want to talk about the trusty pentatonic, which is a great friend of the Aeolian. Let's have a look at the E Minor Pentatonic scale, which is made from the 1st, 3rd, 4th, 5th and 7th intervals of the Aeolian scale (E G A B D).

Example 6g:

This is a cool scale, but often overused, thus it can sound amateurish. When used sparingly and with attitude, however, the pentatonic can sound brutal, even erotic! We can add further *zazz* to the pentatonic by adding a "blue" note – the b5 from the Aeolian scale – which in this case is Bb.

Example 6h:

When used with taste, this subtle outside note can add attitude and quirky tension to an otherwise simple scale.

Arpeggios

Let's talk arpeggios. We can use a simple E Minor triad arpeggio made from the 1st, 3rd and 5th of the Aeolian scale, but this can sound dull and routine. We can make things more sonically colourful by using an Em7 arpeggio (E G B D). Here are Em and Em7 arpeggios side by side.

Example 6i:

Here is an alternative way to play these arpeggios, using the same notes but with a different shape.

Example 6j:

The final arpeggios are six string shapes that cover three octaves. These are a fun way to cover the neck in a diagonal fashion and an excellent way to create drastic intervals and position shifts in improvisation.

Example 6k:

Having alternate shapes of the "same" arpeggio may seem superfluous, but the fact of playing in a different region of the neck often leads to different soloing ideas. It's important to learn multiple different ways to play similar groups of notes. More options mean less restriction and this opens up the fretboard. This in turn will give you limitless freedom that will ultimately lead to further creativity.

Part 4: Aeolian licks to help you get creative

Now let's look at how these ideas can come together in an expressive, musical context.

Example 61 uses the basic E Minor Pentatonic with a classic Chuck Berry entry. The use of bends, legato and slides will make any "meat and veg" blues lick sound instantly more expressive.

Notice that this lick also includes a Bb note (AKA the b5 or devil's tritone). This is the famous "blue" note which creates a moment of sexy blues tension. It is, of course, outside the key signature, so it will sound abrasive and horrendous if you hold it for too long. I tend to play outside notes with slides and quick legato to avoid any sustained, sonic repugnance.

Example 61: E Minor Chuck Berry lick with b5 pull-off roll

This next idea uses a common three-note-per-string E Aeolian scale shape, but I've added in a few legato notes and bends to avoid the monotony of an ascending diatonic scale run.

One of the first things you'll notice about this lick is the massive bend position shifts in the second bar. I've seen Guthrie Govan execute bends like this to quickly jump to a new position on the neck. If you're attempting to create your own licks like this, you can either return to your original position, like I did, or continue playing from the new position established by your second bend. There are no rules! You could even add a third bend if it's in key!

Example 6m: E Aeolian three-note-per-string lick with hammer-ons and shifting position bends

The next lick combines E Minor Pentatonic with a few notes of the E Aeolian diatonic scale. You'll have noticed that blending pentatonic and diatonic scales is a concept I use frequently. I like that you can quickly shift gears from rocky, bluesy good times, to a more emotive diatonic sound. In the example below, this is achieved simply by introducing the second and b6 of the Aeolian scale to create the emotive semitone intervals that the pentatonic cannot.

Example 6n: Ascending E Minor Pentatonic legato lick with descending Aeolian diatonic notes

I'll often use legato and triplets to avoid having a lick only made up of 1/16th notes. You can use this concept in other modal contexts too – just make sure the notes you choose from the diatonic scale are ones that express the flavour of the mode (e.g. the Phrygian's b2 or the Dorian's natural 6th).

This next lick combines a simple ascending E Minor triad arpeggio with an Aeolian diatonic scale descent. I've heard Alexi Laiho and Alex Skolnick use this concept extremely well in a few solos. It adds a nice entry to a descending shred passage. The arpeggio can be slowly picked or hastily swept, depending on your preference. This kind of lick could also be reworked with major, diminished or even augmented arpeggios. Just remain aware of the key signature when playing the diatonic descending part of the lick.

Example 6o: E Minor five-string arpeggio with triplet Aeolian diatonic descent

A few years ago I was listening to a progressive metal band called Scar Symmetry and instantly grew fond of Per Nilsson's playing. There was an amazing arpeggio in one of their songs that blew me away and I've since used it when improvising, not only in metal, but in jazz and blues contexts too. Example 6p combines Per's signature minor eleventh arpeggio shape with some cheeky jazz chromatics and grace notes.

Example 6p: Em11 sliding lick with chromatic notes

This is the kind of lick that sounds great whether played fast or slow. The arpeggio has lots of melodic colour as it covers the 1st, 3rd, 5th, 7th, 9th and 11th intervals of the Em11 chord. The chromatic notes add a quirky, outside sound, and the grace note slide from the "outside" F adds a smooth jazzy flavour to the phrase.

If you get bored of bland arpeggio triads, the addition of the 7th or 9th is a game changer. However, be sparing with the use of chromatics in your playing, as this trick can be easily overused and things will end up sounding too much like *Flight of the Bumblebee.*

Example 6q is another pedal tone idea, using B as our pedal and the notes of E Aeolian. It leads into an E Minor Pentatonic.

Example 6q: Pedal tone E Aeolian lick

Depending on what chords you're playing over, the notes you play against your pedal tone can change according to the progression. You can also vary where you play the pentatonic part of the lick, if a chord change leads you to a different part of the neck. The more you experiment with this lick, the more you'll discover how to apply it. There are no rules other than staying in key and finding a sound you like.

The next example utilises the E Minor Pentatonic scale again and ascends using legato and five-note groupings. It has a sliding note that transitions into a three-string descending Em7 arpeggio.

Example 6r: E Minor Pentatonic third position in fives with three-string Em7 arpeggio

Blending pentatonics and minor arpeggios is an interesting way to bring together bluesy and jazzy sounds. The reason they work together so well is that the pentatonic scale uses the 1st, 3rd, 4th, 5th and 7th intervals of the minor scale; the minor 7th arpeggio uses the same notes but omits the 4th, so they're one note away from having exactly the same notes, while maintaining their own different vibe and flavour.

Example 6s uses two different E Minor Pentatonic positions for its picked and tapped notes. It descends in quick triplets, then ascends in sixteenths through the scale. It ends with an outside bend from D# to E.

You'll notice I'm pretty obsessed with outside bends and I love ending licks with them. Players like Marty Friedman, Nick Johnston and Guthrie Govan use this technique frequently. It's one way of playing technical, exciting phrases but still adding an element of tension and emotion.

Example 6s: E Minor Pentatonic with taps and sliding position shift

The next lick uses a pretty basic five-string E Minor triad arpeggio, but changes the note order to create a more interesting pattern. This is a quick way to make the arpeggio sound more like a phrase than a linear "textbook" arpeggio.

You'll also notice I've added in some legato and slides, just to force position shifts. Often, playing a passage of notes on just one string using slides is a great "storytelling" technique to add to your lead playing. There's a small lead line in the Iron Maiden epic *Fear of the Dark* that occurs just before the main solos that perfectly illustrates the art of storytelling on guitar.

Example 6t: Skipping interval E Minor arpeggio lick with slides

The final lick in this chapter is a G Ionian string skip lick. Because we are operating in the same key signature as E Aeolian, I promise it's safe to use! The lick shifts between 1/8th note and 1/16th note triplets to add speed and an element of surprise. The use of string skips creates more interesting intervals and at times can sound a bit like an arpeggio.

Example 6u: G Ionian string skip legato lick

Everything you've learned to play in E Aeolian can be modulated to other Aeolian (Natural Minor) keys. As ever, seek out some backing tracks to jam to and keep in mind that Aeolian is the saddest mode of all. Keep a box of tissues handy in case your emotions get out of hand!

Chapter 7: Elusive Locrian

The final chapter of our modal journey is a scary and elusive one. We'll end our adventure by plunging into a dark, mysterious, murky forest. It's likely that the forest is riddled with ghouls and hobgoblins (I probably should've warned you about that). There is an ice-cream truck that only sells liquorice and orange flavours and has an iPod playlist consisting solely of Black Sabbath, Diamond Head and Slayer playing on repeat over a loud speaker. Now you are fully immersed in the mystery and tension that is the Locrian mode.

For many years I was fearful and dismissive of this scary, elusive mode. On many occasions I said to my students, "Don't worry about the Locrian, it's awful. It's almost IMPOSSIBLE to make it sound good." Until very recently I would have stood by those words, but now, as an older, wiser man of thirty-one and a half, I'm here to tell you that the Locrian is a super-interesting mode with tension, allure and subtlety.

The thing that fascinates me the most about the Locrian is that it can sound so poignantly evil. So evil that it has the potential to conjure demons faster than a common household Ouija board (yes, we all have one in the attic). Yet, it also has a tense, jazz-fusion sound to it, which makes it the well-kept secret that most players don't know about.

The Locrian mode is, of course, the last of our seven diatonic modes, which to refresh your memory are: Ionian, Dorian, Phrygian, Lydian, Mixolydian, Aeolian and Locrian – the most evil of all modes.

Part 1: Finding the Locrian sound

In this chapter we will use A Locrian for all our examples. Let's look at the A Locrian scale in one octave.

Example 7a:

Locrian has a dark and dangerous vibe, and of course should be learn as an isolated sound. However, once again, it's useful to have other perspectives in the back of our mind.

Locrian is…

1. The seventh mode of the major scale.

2. An Aeolian (Natural Minor) scale with a b2 and b5 (the latter is often referred to as the diminished 5th).

Let's take a look at A Aeolian and A Locrian side by side:

A Aeolian = A B C D E F G A

A Locrian = A Bb C D Eb F G A

Example 7b:

Aeolian scale formula = 1 2 b3 4 5 b6 b7

Locrian scale formula = 1 b2 b3 4 b5 b6 b7

When displayed side by side, you can see there are two notes in the Locrian mode that stand out like a gangsta rapper in a kilt shop. It's the b2 (Bb) and b5 (Eb) that make the Locrian sound more nasty and gross than the inoffensive Aeolian mode.

It's crucial that we highlight these two important notes to bring out the full flavour of the Locrian.

The harsh intervals of the b2 and b5 can be heard in the chord progression example below. Play through the chords and the ascending and descending Locrian scale variations straight after to hear the unsettling, abrasive nature of this scale in a melodic and musical context.

Example 7c: A Locrian chord progression with scale ascend & descend

Scale Runs

```
T--------------------------5--7----5-------------------------------5--7----5-------
A------------5--6--8-----------------8--6--5-----------5--6--8-----------------8--6--5---
B--5--6--8-------------------------------8--6--5---5--6--8-----------------------------8--6--5--
```

The characteristic b2, Bb note is present in the Bb Major chord, which is quite similar to the tense nature of the b2 we previously saw in Phrygian mode, especially when you hear its interplay with the chords. The other Locrian characteristic note is the b5, Eb note, which can be heard in the Am7b5, C Minor and Bb Major chord. It has a tense, devil-summoning sound that we hear a lot in evilest of heavy metal songs.

As I've mentioned in previous chapters, scale theory and interval knowledge will only take you so far. To further understand the Locrian mode, here's few Locrian songs for you to check out:

• Painkiller – Judas Priest

• Juicebox – The Strokes

• Blackened – Metallica

• Raining Blood (chorus section 1:39) – Slayer

Part 2: The Locrian diatonic chords

Throughout this book I have REPEATEDLY discussed the importance of knowing the diatonic chords within a key or mode. I'm sorry for sounding like such a broken record. Believe me, I get it! Personally, nothing makes me more infuriated than having to sit through one of my dad's stories that he told me only three days ago (though he thinks it's the first time). More so having to pretend that it's just as funny as the first time (breathes heavily into paper bag). Sorry, I had to get that out of my system. I still get night terrors from time to time from all the fake smiles and forced laughter.

That said, understanding the diatonic chords and their function will help you determine how to bring out each mode's unique flavour. The relationship between the i chord and bII chord creates the characteristic semitone tension of the Locrian, while the i and bV chord have the tritone tension. When these tense chord relationships are used in a chord progression, the signature Locrian sound comes out. Let's look at the Locrian diatonic chords compared to that of the Ionian mode.

Diatonic chords starting from chord 1 (Ionian)

maj	min	min	maj	maj	min	min7b5 (or 1/2 diminished)
I	ii	iii	IV	V	vi	vii

Diatonic chords starting from chord 7 (Locrian)

min7b5	maj	min	min	maj	maj	min
i	bII	biii	iv	bV	bVI	bvii

A Locrian is the 7th mode of Bb Major as both scales share the same number of flats. This means we can simply reorder the diatonic chords of Bb Ionian starting from the vii chord to give us the A Locrian chord structure.

Example 7d:

To highlight the unique Locrian sound in a chord progression we will want to focus on the b2 and b5 notes of the mode. The combination of the i and bII chord gives us the *Jaws* sound (similar to the Phrygian). Introducing the bV chord gives us the tritone tension that is also found in the Lydian mode. The bII and bV chords have the root notes Bb and Eb respectively – both Locrian character notes.

Bb Major (bII chord) = Bb D F

Eb Major (bV chord) = Eb G Bb

Try writing a few chord progressions with the Locrian chords, preferably starting and ending on the Am7b5 chord. Here are two ideas to start you off:

Example 7e – Progression 1:

94

Example 7f – Progression 2:

Part 3: Soloing in Locrian with scales and arpeggios

When I solo modally, I feel more confident if I have a wide range of options. In the case of the Locrian, we'll approach it in the same way as the previous modes, with the three big questions:

1. What is a three-note-per-string version of the scale from the root?

2. What kind of pentatonics can I use e.g. regular, custom or relative minor?

3. What kind of arpeggios will bring out the flavour of the mode?

With the Locrian, bear in mind that the b2 and b5 are somewhat problematic intervals. In other words, you'll see some weird scale shapes you may not have seen before!

Let's look at the A Locrian three-note-per-string scale shape. This is the fastest, most effective way to hear the Locrian mode spanning two and a bit octaves. It's also super easy to use in a shred or legato context!

Example 7g:

Pentatonics

The next scale we'll look at is a pentatonic specially designed to deal with the pesky Locrian mode. I call it "pesky" because the Locrian mode it is completely devoid of a natural 5th.

The scale formula for a regular minor pentatonic is 1, b3, 4, 5 and b7, but this doesn't work for the Locrian. If we want to use pentatonic ideas for the Locrian we will have to use the 1 b3, 4, b5 and b7 to cooperate with the chords and key signature. A Locrian's "custom pentatonic" notes are therefore A, C, D, Eb and G.

Let's have a look at the A Minor Pentatonic scale (1 b3 4 5 b7) and an A Locrian pentatonic scale (1 b3 4 b5 b7) side by side:

Example 7h:

Now let's view these scales in multiple positions across the fretboard. In effect we are playing all the remaining A Minor Pentatonic shapes and flattening the 5th (E to Eb).

Example 7i:

Arpeggios

Finally, let's look at our arpeggio soloing options. Due to the fact that the Locrian mode is so heavily rooted in the minor7b5 chord, we're going to look at multiple sexy ways to play this arpeggio with A Locrian.

The first arpeggio we'll look at is two variations of a five-string Am7b5 arpeggio (A C Eb G). If you wish, you can add hammer-ons on any of the strings that have two notes.

Example 7j:

You'll notice that on the first Am7b5 arpeggio shape, the order of the notes has been rearranged to G A C and Eb. We're essentially leading the arpeggio from the seventh instead of the root.

I also use this "leading seventh" approach when playing major, minor and dominant arpeggios. Beginning on the seventh then playing the root soon after creates a nice moment of tension. It's not a rule – just something I'm partial to. You may find you like this approach too. To quote the 80s rock powerhouse Roxette, "Listen to your heart"!

The final arpeggio shape we'll look at is a six-string Am7b5 arpeggio that spans three octaves. Once again we will lead from the seventh of the arpeggio in each octave.

Example 7k:

Keep in mind that these m7b5 arpeggio shapes can be used in any Locrian key, provided you move the root note to correctly modulate to the desired key. You can also try these shapes over the vii chord in any Ionian progression or any time a m7b5 chord comes up.

Another fact of great interest (to me at least – yes, I am a massive nerd!) is that m7b5 arpeggios can be superimposed over ii and V chords in major keys. For example, in the key of G Major, we can play an F#m7b5 arpeggio (F# A C E) over an Am or Am7 ii chord, as it has exactly the same notes as the triad, plus the major 6th, thus bringing out a momentary Dorian inference, and also suggesting an Am6 chord. We can also play an F#m7b5 arpeggio over a D7 V chord (D F# A C). Over this latter chord, it has the effect of creating a dominant ninth sound.

Part 4: Locrian licks to help you get creative

If you've got this far, you've done really well. You know by now that in part four of a chapter we take all the scale shapes and arpeggios from part three and turn them into an array of sexy licks and useable melodic ideas. This chapter is no exception, but I must warn you … some of these licks are pretty *redonkulous!*

This first lick uses the first position of the A Locrian pentatonic. We'll be highlighting the b5 (because we have to!) which will result in a familiar bluesy sound.

Example 7l: A Locrian pentatonic position 1 bluesy lick

The next lick uses the three-note-per-string A Locrian shape. We ascend the scale and add in a few hammer-ons for effect and to vary the timing. This lick ends with an outside-to-inside bend.

Example 7m: A Locrian three-note-per-string ascending shred lick with legato and outside-inside bend

The next example uses the second position of A Locrian pentatonic. We'll ascend using multiple hammer-ons and strange note groupings, but keep to a consistent 1/16th note pulse. The lick resolves with a slide into a descending Am7b5 arpeggio.

Example 7n: A Locrian pentatonic position two with m7b5 arpeggio descent

Example 7o uses the combination of an Am7b5 arpeggio and an Eb Major arpeggio with a perfect 4th across two octaves. Each arpeggio is played in an ascending manner with taps.

This lick is an interesting alternative to a linear, one-string tap lick, or a standard ascending triad arpeggio, or swept arpeggio. As you've probably guessed, this concept is not limited to this mode. If you swap around the notes to suit the key you're in, the possibilities are limitless, so get experimenting!

Example 7o: A Locrian two octave tap lick

Example 7p ascends through a five string Am7b5 arpeggio using a triplet pulse. Then it descends through a D Phrygian three-note-per-string scale shape. Pay close attention to the hammer-on placement and cheeky slide at the end of the lick

Example 7p: Five-string Am7b5 arpeggio with D Phrygian diatonic descent

The next lick uses the diatonic A Locrian scale in an ascending manner, but I've mixed up the order of the notes to keep things interesting. The note order in the lick is 1st, 3rd, 2nd, 5th, 7th and 6th, and this repeats over two octaves. I've also used dotted 1/8th notes and regular 1/16th notes to make the timing more interesting and less predictable.

Example 7q: Diagonal 1 3 2 5 7 6 Locrian crawling lick

Here is an idea based on moving swept three-string diminished arpeggios. The idea of moving the same lick up the fretboard in minor 3rds (three semitones) has been done to death. If possible, it's even more offensive when performed with diminished harmony! But, due to the fact that we're not in a harmonic minor key, we can use multiple Am7b5 arpeggio shapes that change in every position!

Example 7r: Three-string multiple position Am7b5 arpeggio

You will notice that once again, I ended this lick with an outside note, bent a semitone to a scale note. I know, I have a problem, but I'm going to get help.

Here is the A Locrian pentatonic ascending in five-note groupings. This lick is played with lots of legato to make it smoother and more "loosey goosey"!

Example 7s: A Locrian pentatonic position three with five-note groupings lick

Now we come to another pedal tone idea – this time using a mid-register "A" note against which we ascend the notes of the A Locrian scale. The lick has a triplet pulse and moves into an ascending Am7b5 arpeggio.

Example 7t: Pedal A Locrian lick with Am7b5 arpeggio

The final example uses two octaves of the six-string Am7b5 shape illustrated in part three. It consists mostly of 1/16th notes with the occasional legato triplet to mix up the rhythm. It ends by descending an A Locrian pentatonic box pattern.

Example 7u: Am7b5 two octave arpeggio with Locrian pentatonic descent

As you know, everything in this chapter can be transferred to other Locrian keys or used in passing over any m7b5 chord that presents itself in a chord progression.

Epilogue & Acknowledgements

I would like to thank the many students I've had over the years, who were with me during my studies and musical journey. You all pushed me to be the best musical version of myself and I'm eternally grateful.

Thanks to the friends I've made in the Melbourne music scene and through YouTube – you have all been an enormous support and have inspired me in my writing and performance. Most importantly, you've helped get me out of my horrendous and often inescapable introvert bubble.

Finally, I want to thank my beautiful wife, Lucie, my son, Alexi, and my cat, Andrew P. Rodriguez. You are the lights in my life. You all manage to make me smile every day, and everything I achieve is with your help, encouragement and love.

Other Books from Fundamental Changes

The Complete Guide to Playing Blues Guitar Book One: Rhythm Guitar

The Complete Guide to Playing Blues Guitar Book Two: Melodic Phrasing

The Complete Guide to Playing Blues Guitar Book Three: Beyond Pentatonics

The Complete Guide to Playing Blues Guitar Compilation

The CAGED System and 100 Licks for Blues Guitar

Minor ii V Mastery for Jazz Guitar

Jazz Blues Soloing for Guitar

Guitar Scales in Context

Guitar Chords in Context

The First 100 Chords for Guitar

Jazz Guitar Chord Mastery

Complete Technique for Modern Guitar

Funk Guitar Mastery

The Complete Technique, Theory & Scales Compilation for Guitar

Sight Reading Mastery for Guitar

Rock Guitar Un-CAGED

The Practical Guide to Modern Music Theory for Guitarists

Beginner's Guitar Lessons: The Essential Guide

Chord Tone Soloing for Jazz Guitar

Chord Tone Soloing for Bass Guitar

Voice Leading Jazz Guitar

Guitar Fretboard Fluency

The Circle of Fifths for Guitarists

First Chord Progressions for Guitar

The First 100 Jazz Chords for Guitar

100 Country Licks for Guitar

Pop & Rock Ukulele Strumming

Walking Bass for Jazz and Blues

Guitar Finger Gym

The Melodic Minor Cookbook

The Chicago Blues Guitar Method

Heavy Metal Rhythm Guitar

Heavy Metal Lead Guitar

Progressive Metal Guitar

Heavy Metal Guitar Bible

Exotic Pentatonic Soloing for Guitar

The Complete Jazz Guitar Soloing Compilation

The Jazz Guitar Chords Compilation

Fingerstyle Blues Guitar

The Complete DADGAD Guitar Method

Country Guitar for Beginners

Beginner Lead Guitar Method

The Country Fingerstyle Guitar Method

Beyond Rhythm Guitar

Rock Rhythm Guitar Playing

Fundamental Changes in Jazz Guitar

Neo-Classical Speed Strategies for Guitar

100 Classic Rock Licks for Guitar

The Beginner's Guitar Method Compilation

100 Classic Blues Licks for Guitar

The Country Guitar Method Compilation

Country Guitar Soloing Techniques

Ultimate Shred Machine by Chris Zoupa

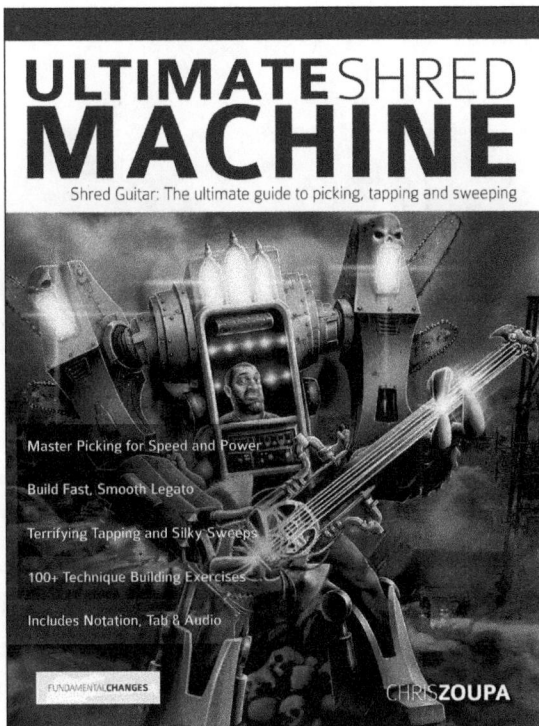

Ultimate Shred Machine: Shred Guitar: The ultimate guide to picking, tapping and sweeping

• A no-nonsense guide to essential rock guitar techniques

• Master alternate picking, legato, tapping and sweeping

• Over 100 exercises and licks with FREE supporting audio

The ultimate guide to mastering shred guitar technique with Chris Zoupa

Forget vanilla 'safe space' guides and make way for the Ultimate Shred Machine – the ultimate guide to shred guitar picking, tapping and sweeping!

In this no-nonsense guide to shred guitar, seasoned teacher and YouTube sensation Chris Zoupa cuts through the mystery and misinformation that shrouds guitar technique, and expertly guides you through the essential skills that'll super-charge your rock guitar playing.

Drawing from a rich tapestry of shred guitar techniques, and the styles of the players who have made them famous, Ultimate Shred Machine is a solid foundation of virtuoso guitar technique and picks up where other guitar methods stop.

What you'll learn:

• How to play flawless shred guitar, taught in an easy-to-follow manner

• The secrets of fast alternate picking guitar technique

• How to sweep-pick arpeggios the right way and avoid common mistakes

• Legato guitar technique in the styles of Satriani, Govan and Gilbert

• Exotic scale runs in the styles of Malmsteen, Skolnick and Laiho

• Neo-classical metal guitar exercises and licks

• Simple to advanced guitar tapping techniques

• Over 100 exercises and guitar licks with FREE supporting audio to download

• Great tips on guitar tone and the use of distortion

www.ingramcontent.com/pod-product-compliance
Lightning Source LLC
Chambersburg PA
CBHW081431090426
42740CB00017B/3266